Oceans of Color
By Robin Joy Andreae

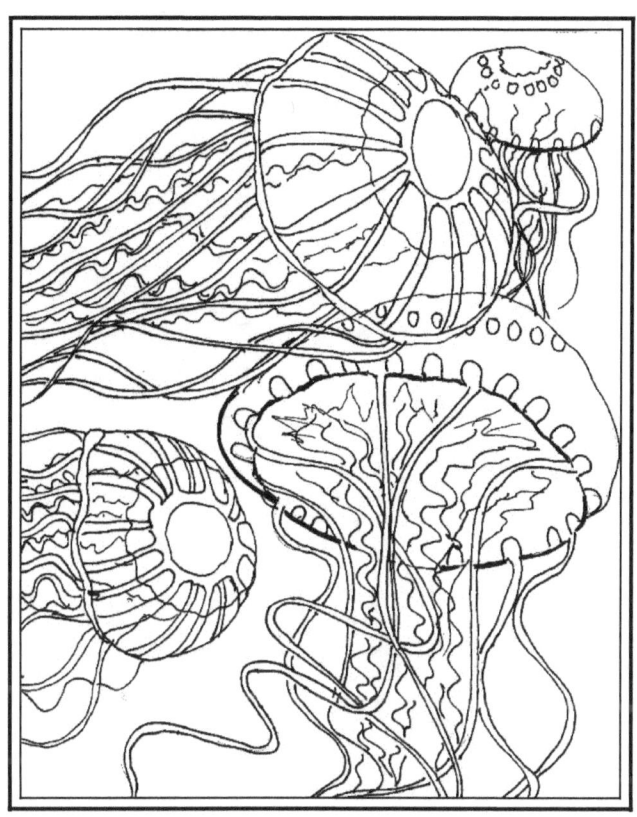

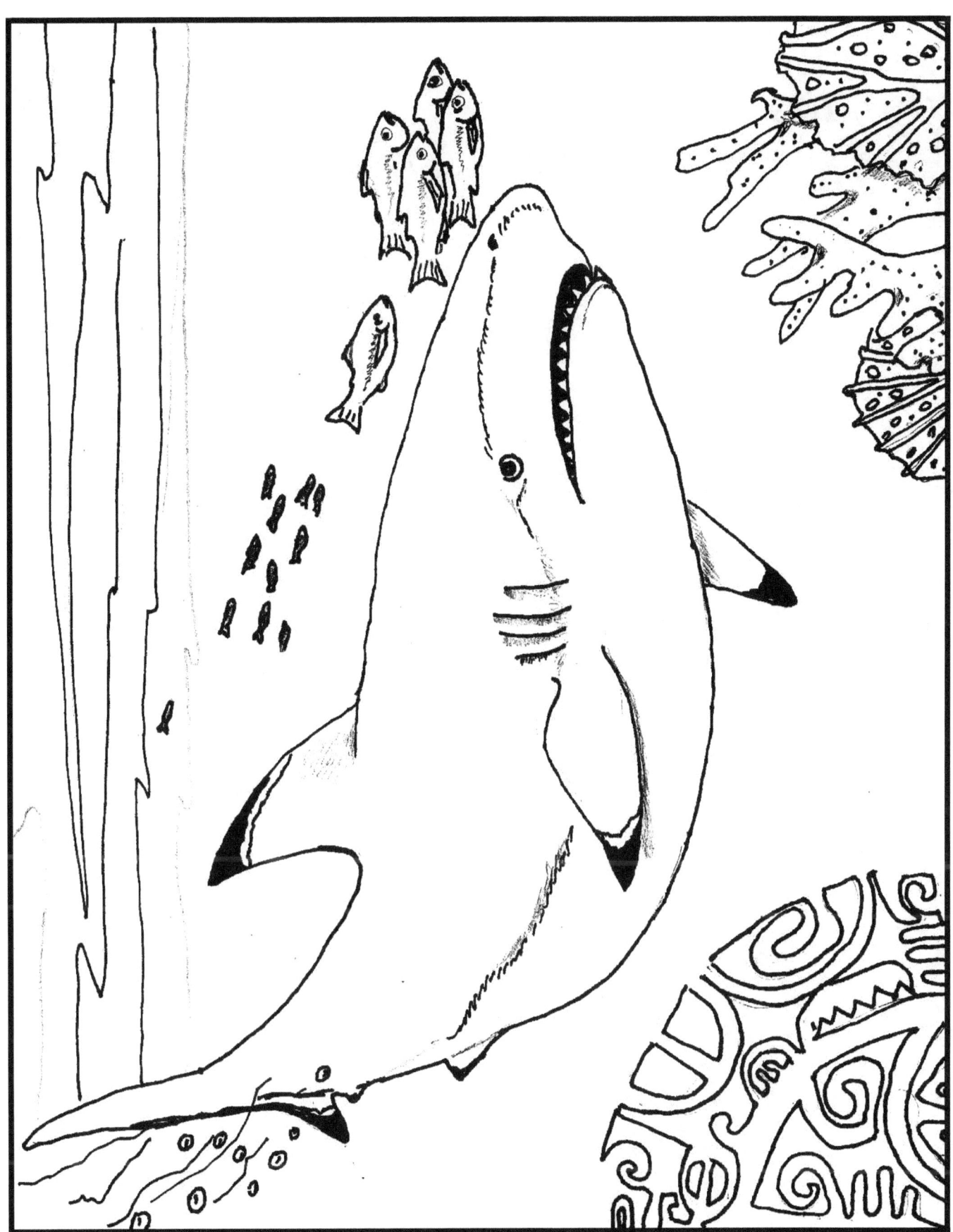

Figure 1 Black Tipped Shark

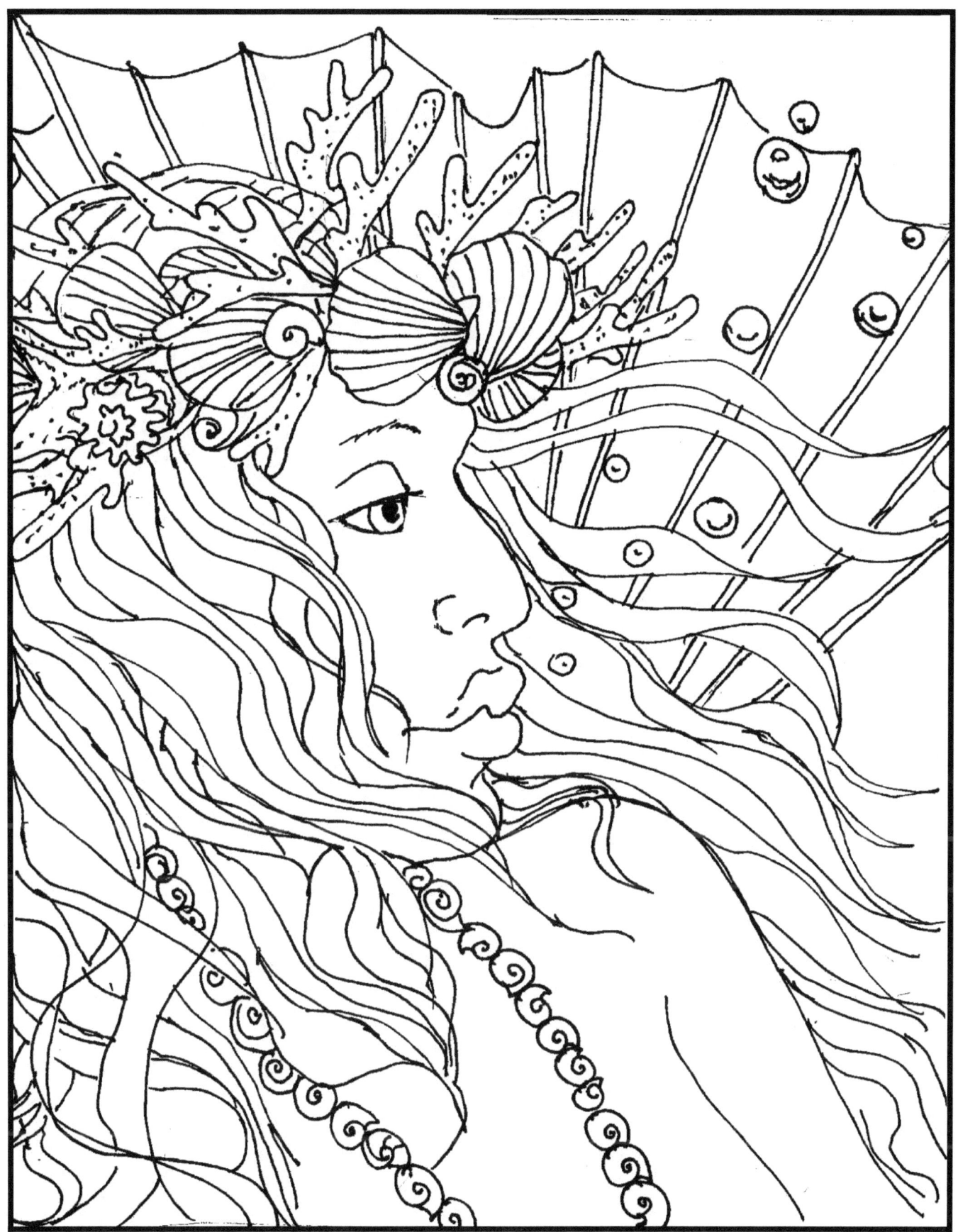

Figure 2 Mermaid

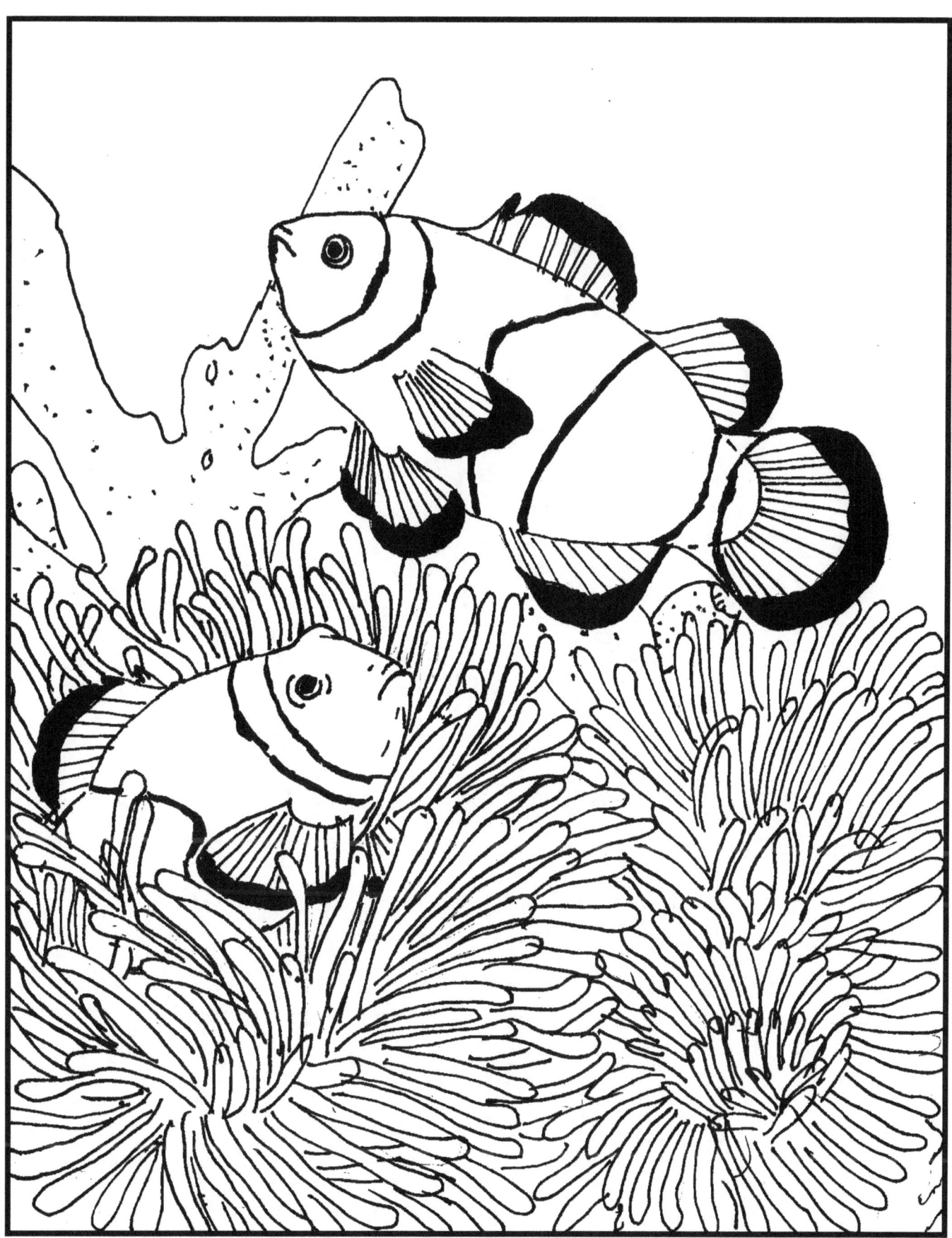

Figure 3 Clown Fish

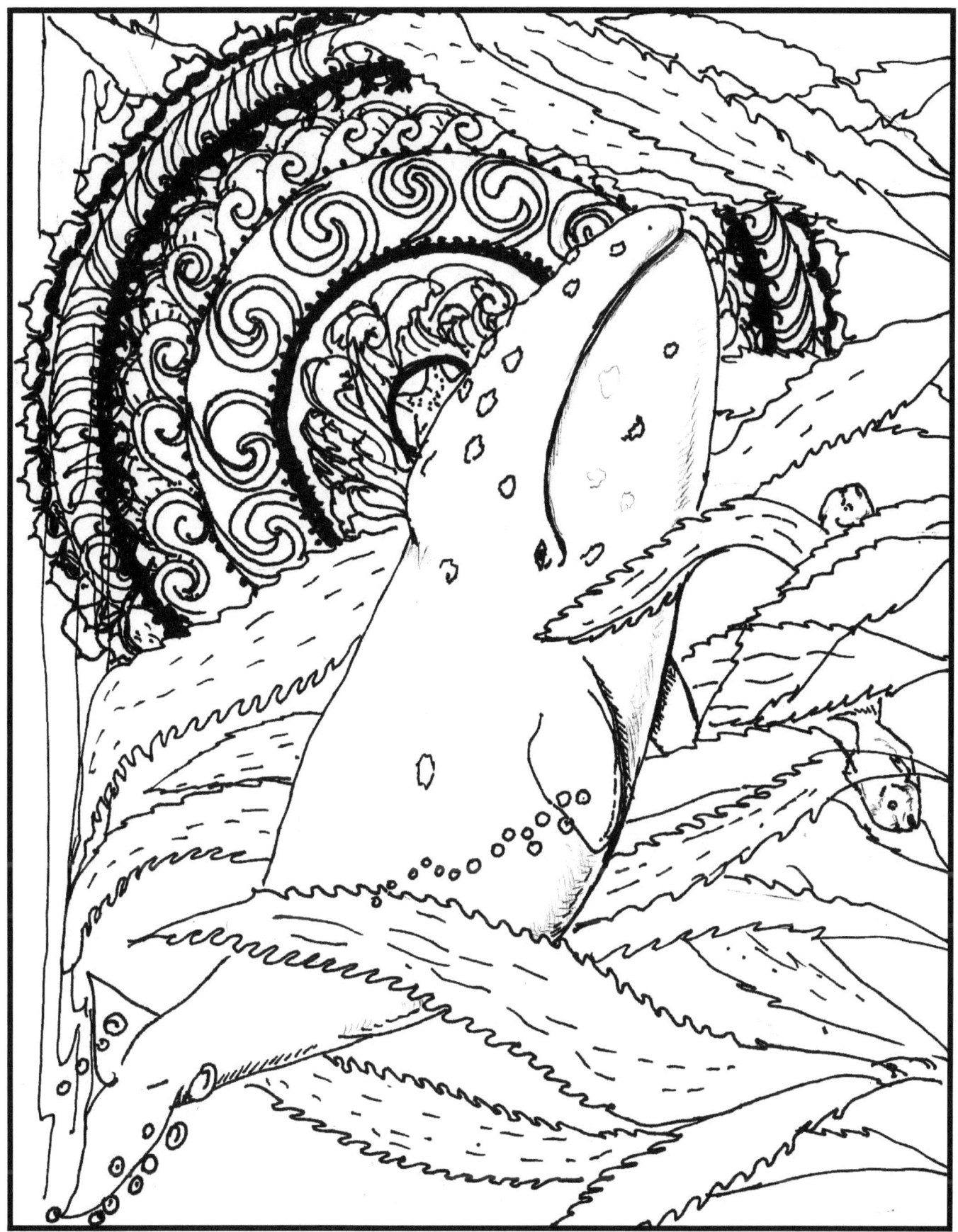

Figure 4 California Gray Whale

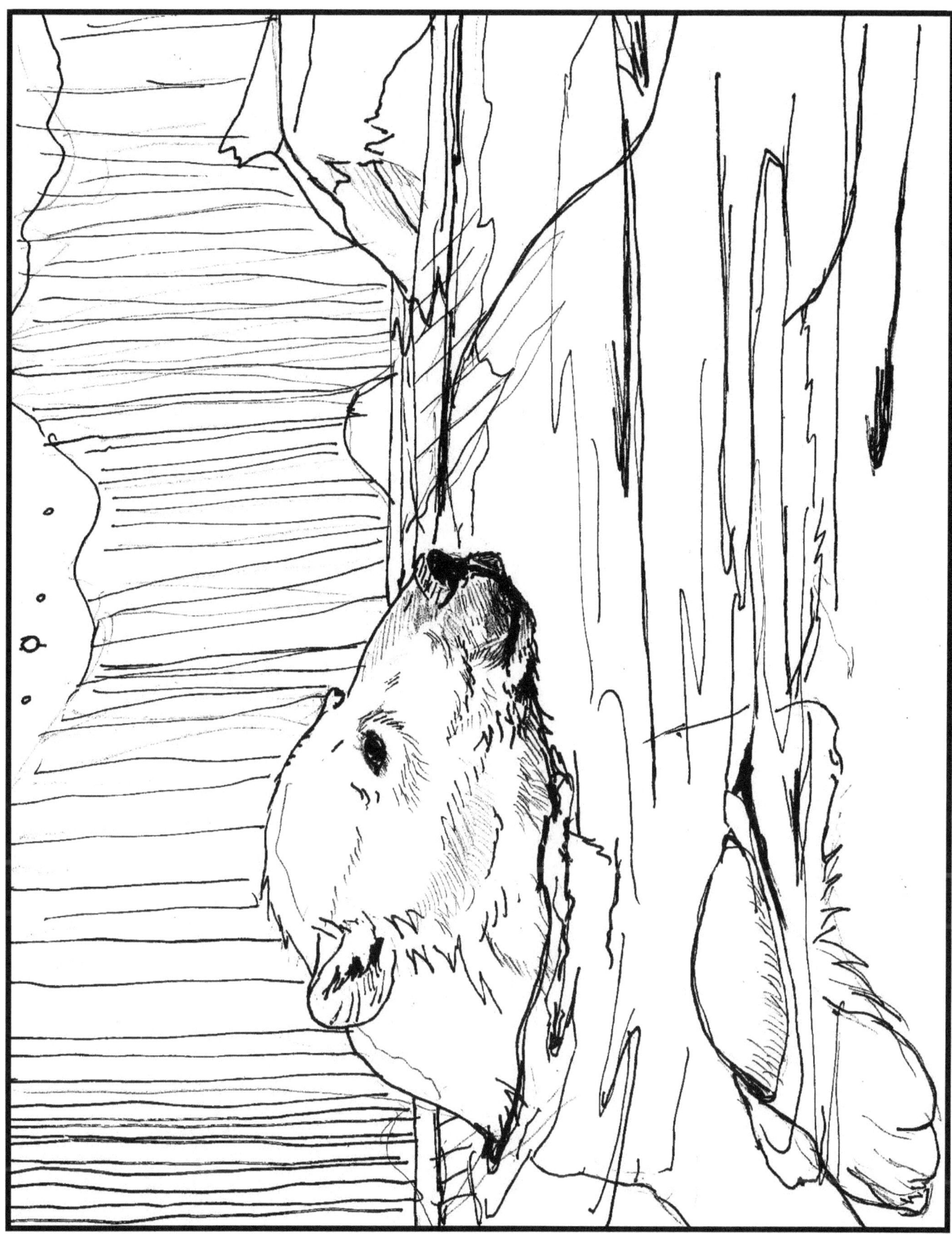

Figure 5 Polar Bear

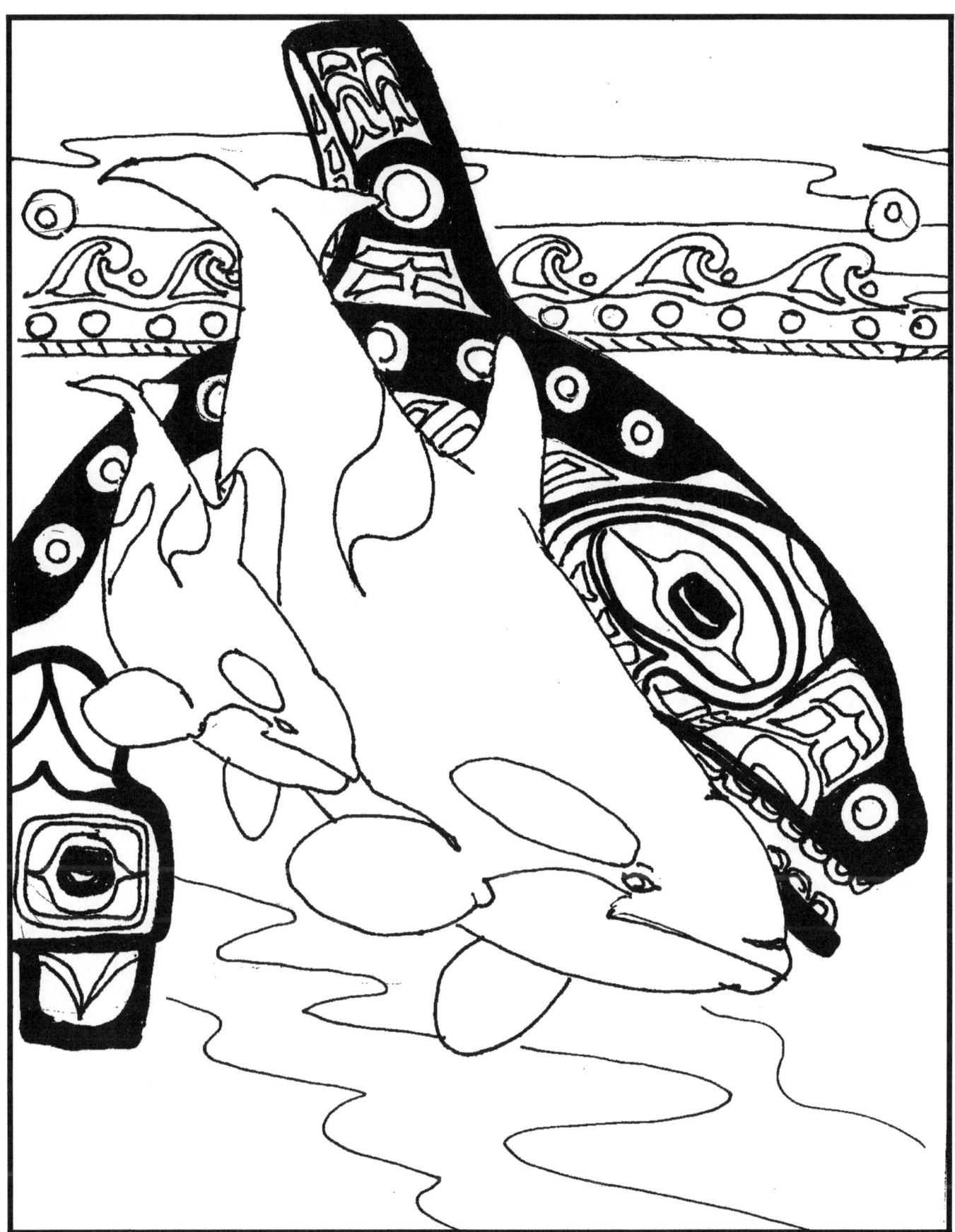

Figure 6 Orcas

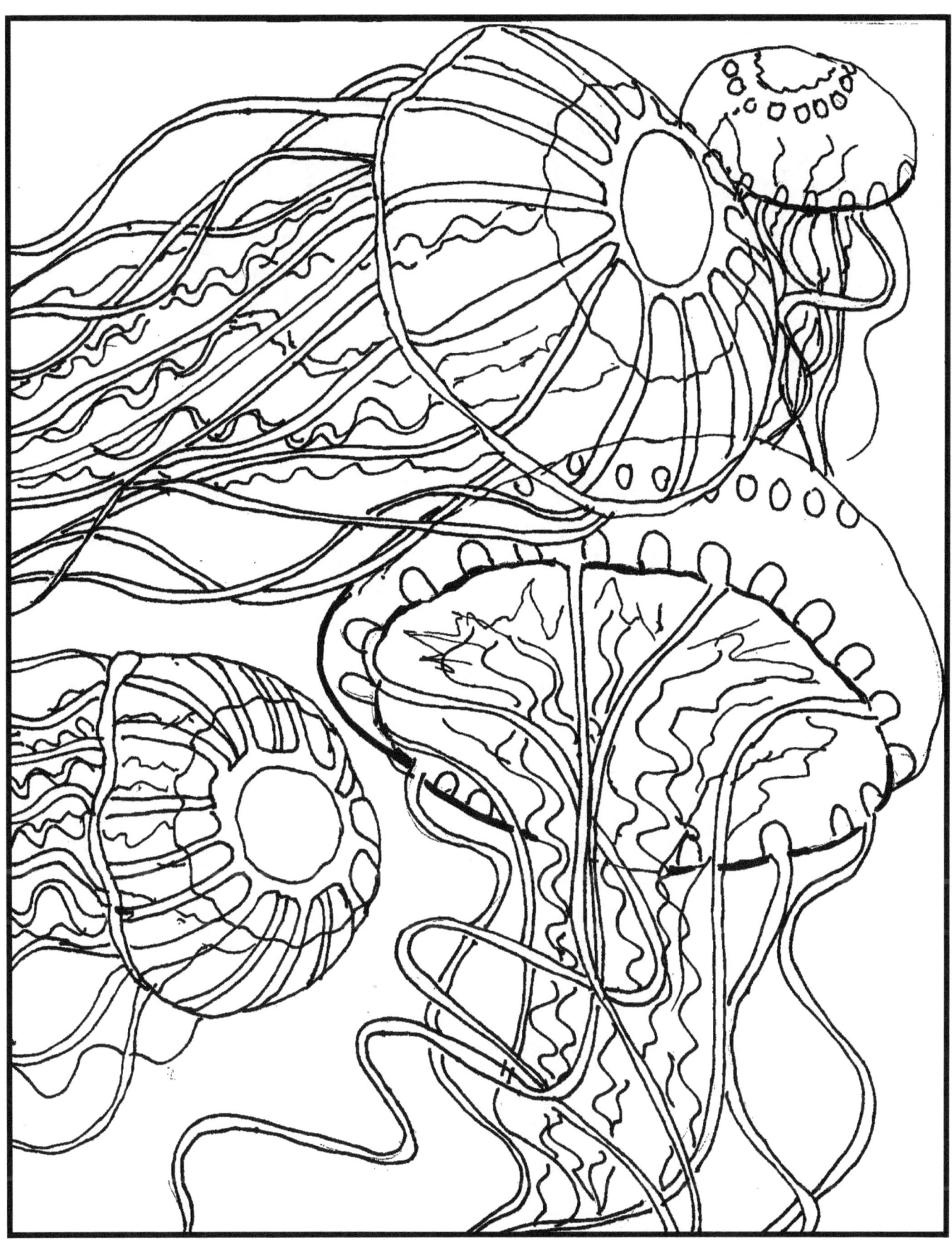

Figure 7 Jellyf

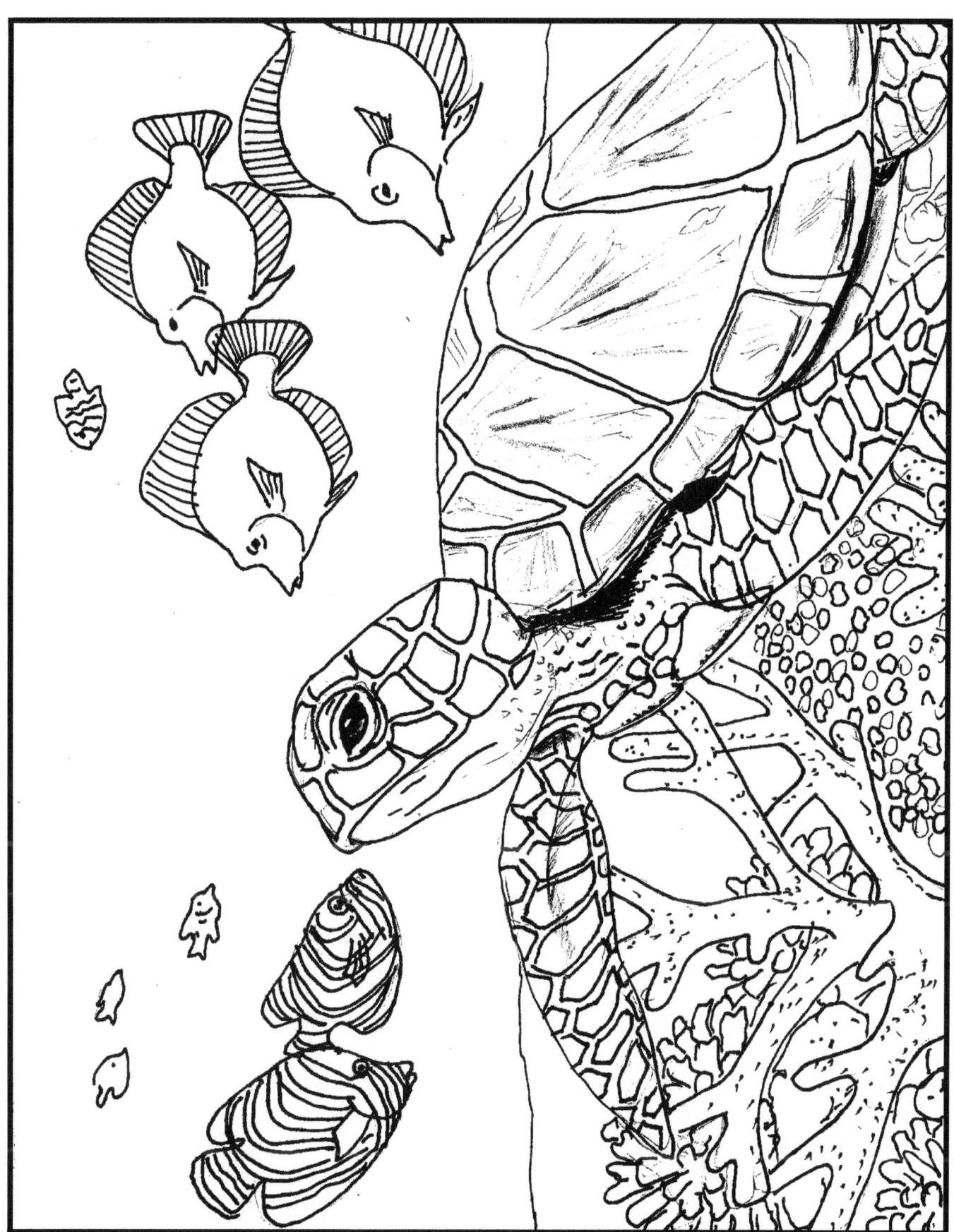

Figure 8 Sea Turtle

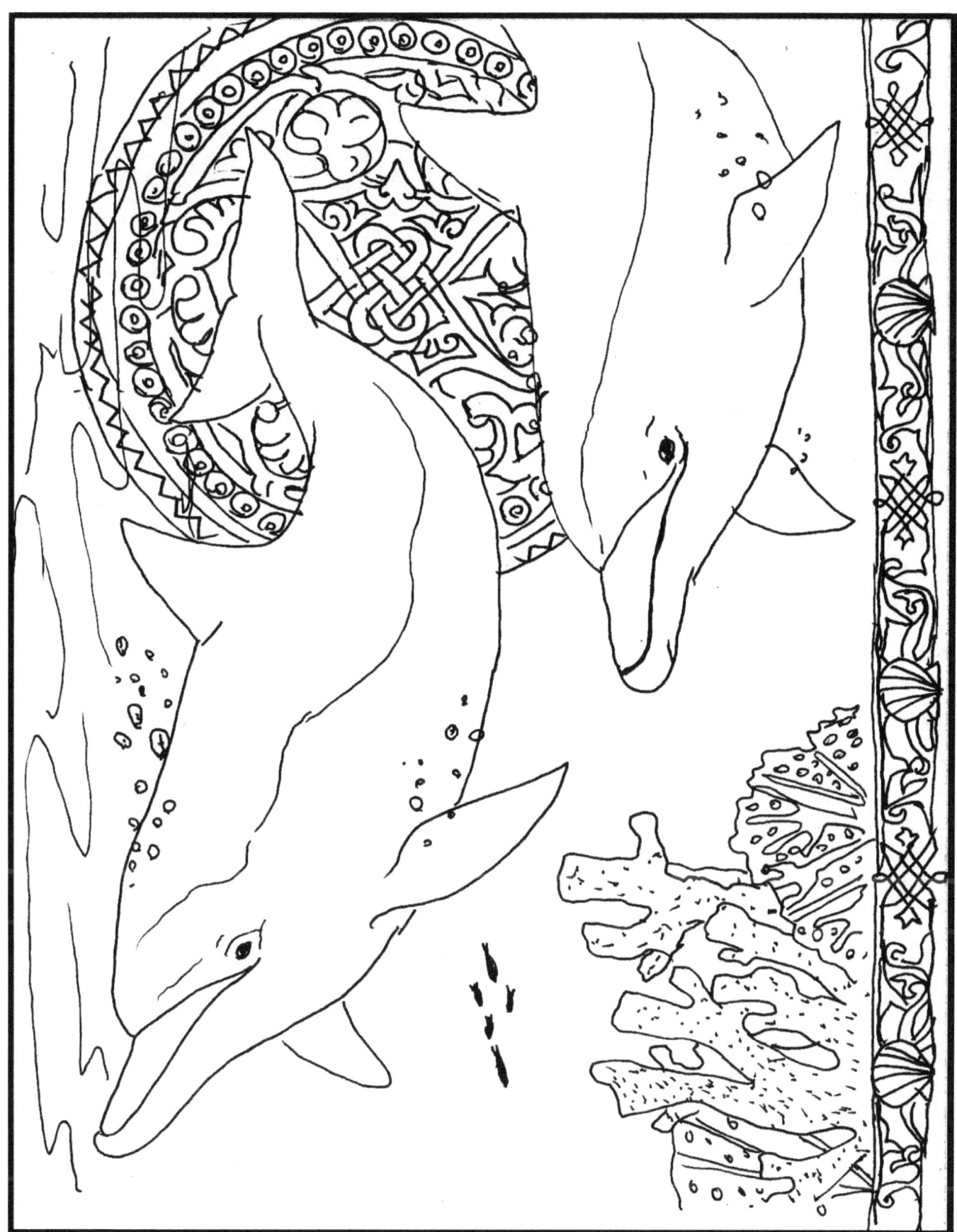

Figure 9 Bottlenose Dolphins

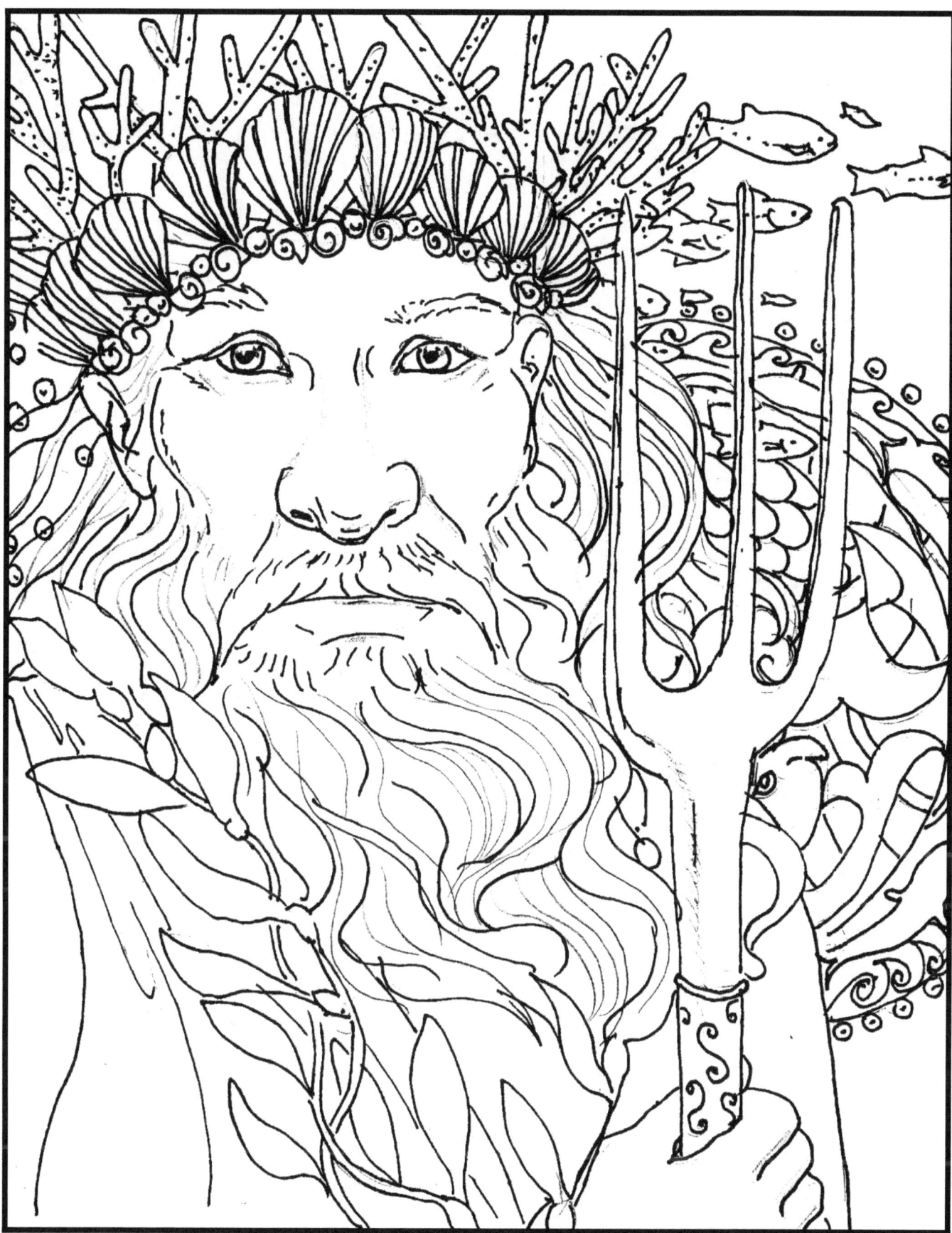

Figure 10 Poseidon

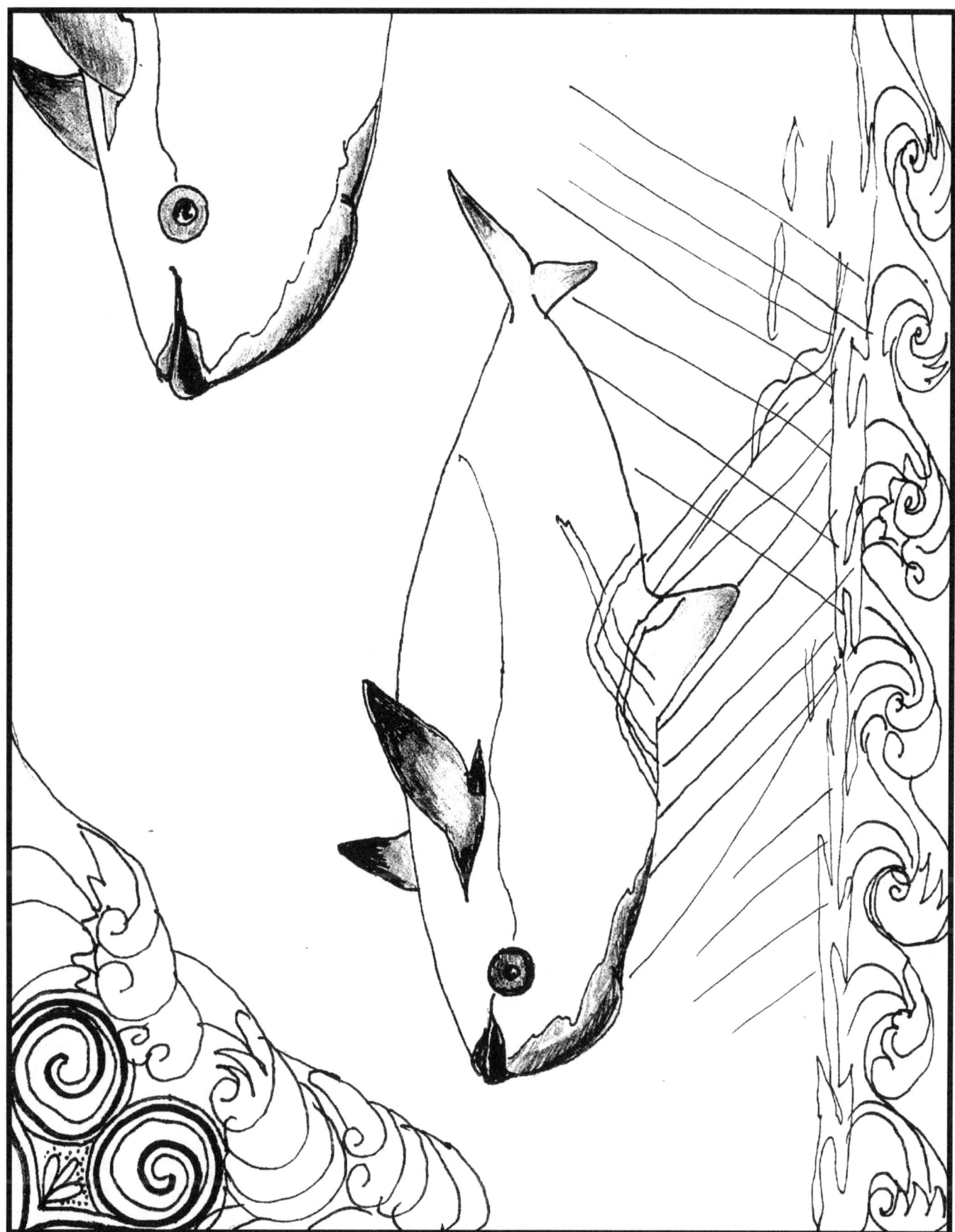

Figure 11 Vaquitas

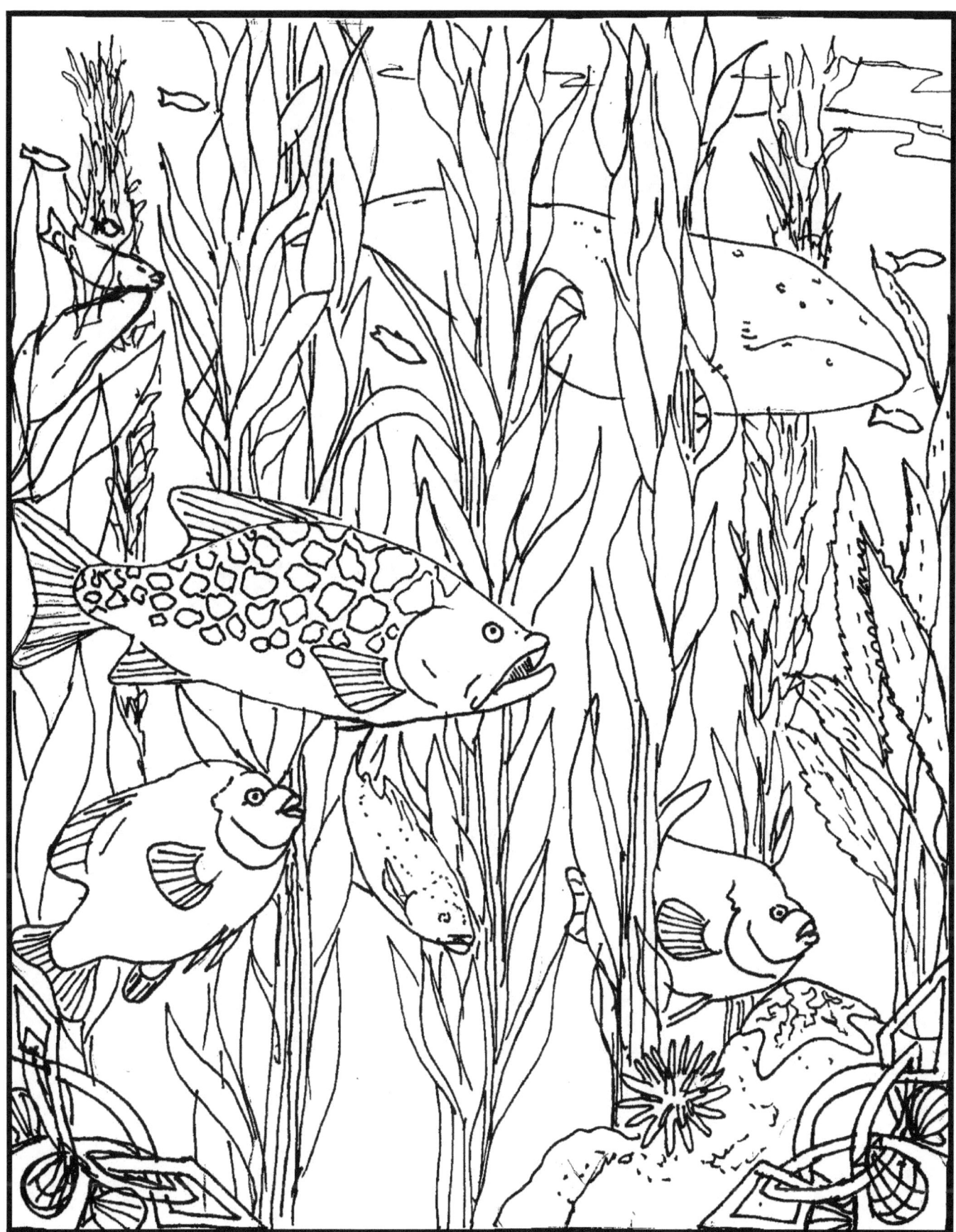

Figure 12 Kelp Forest

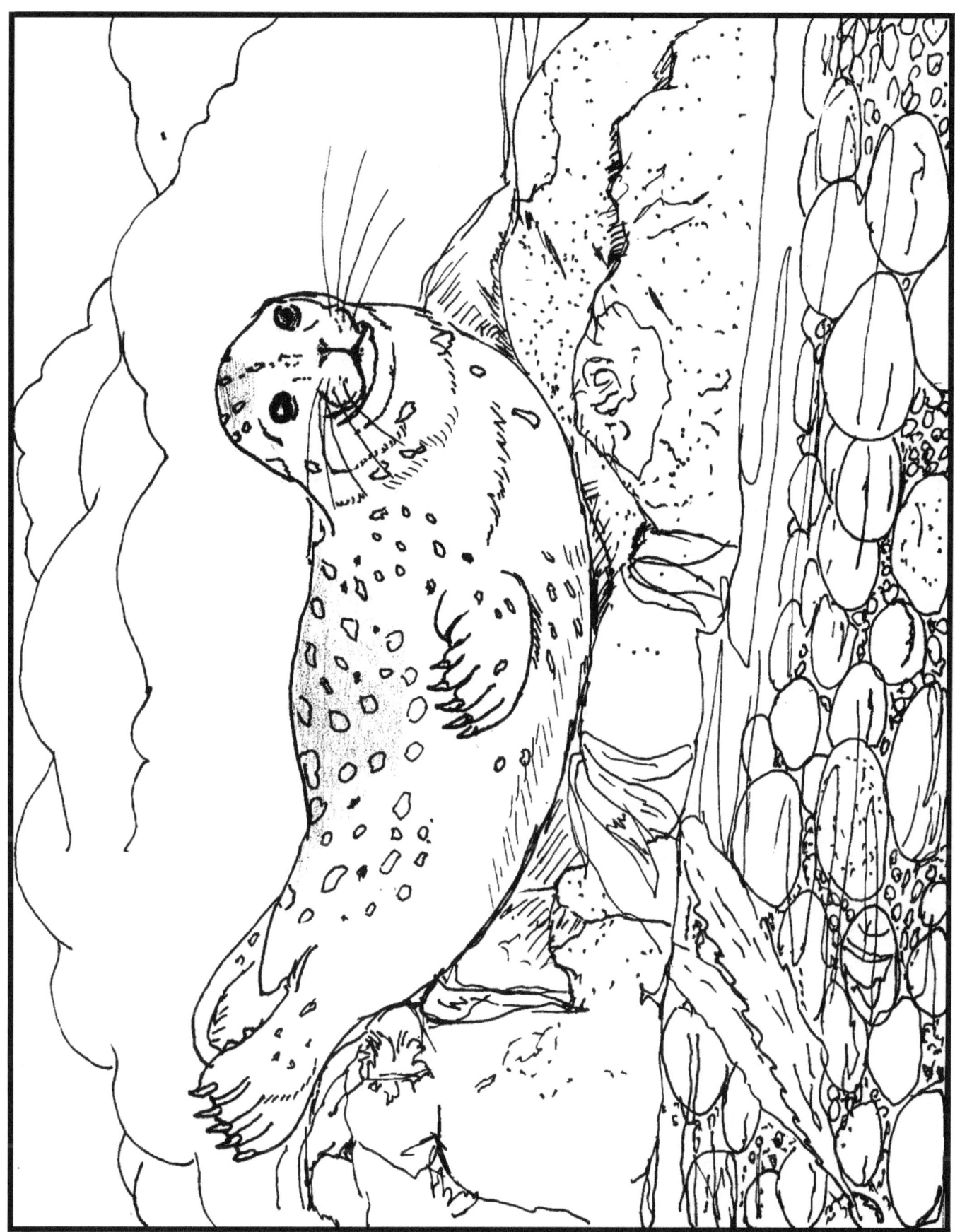

Figure 13 Harbor Seal

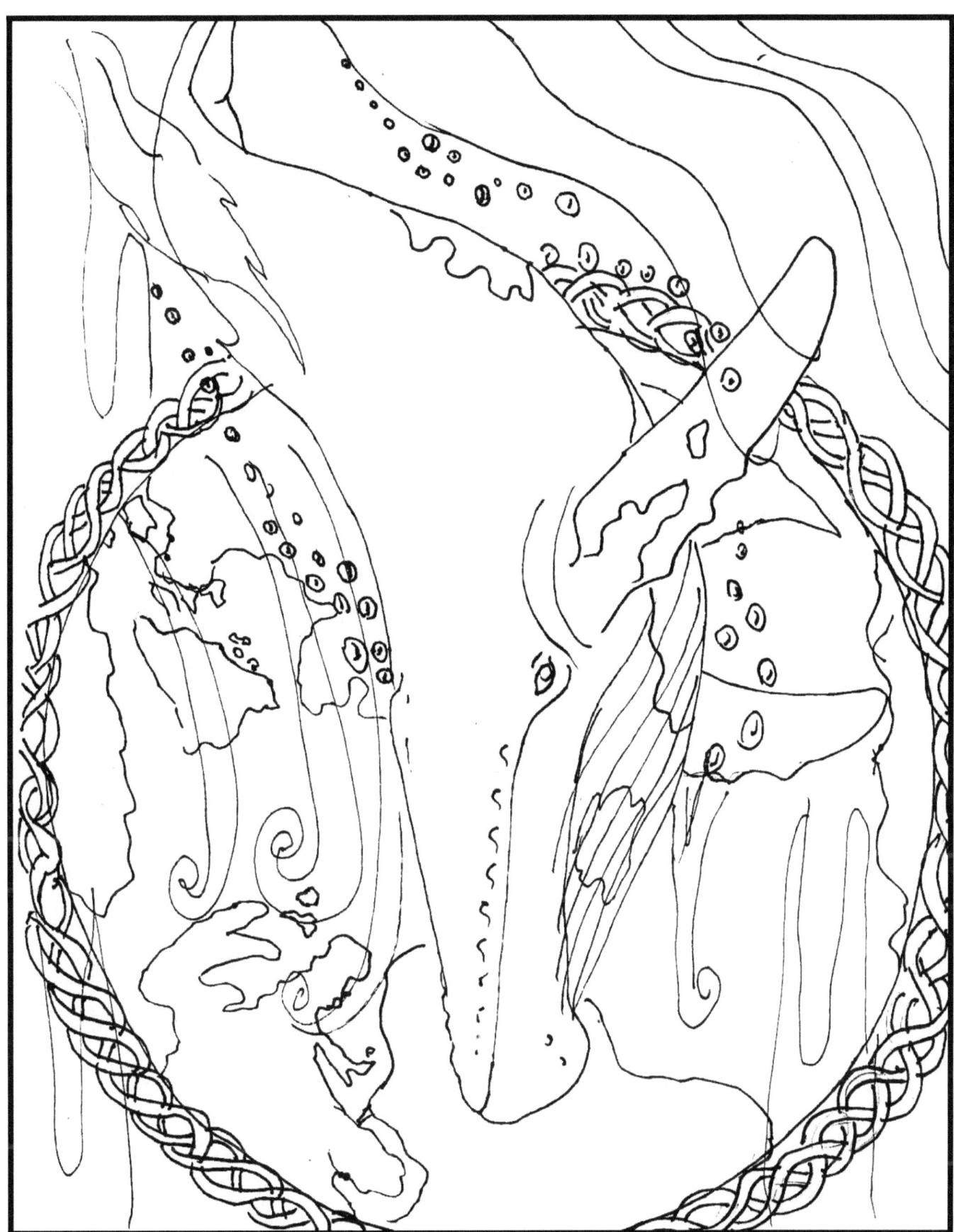

Figure 14 Humpback Whale

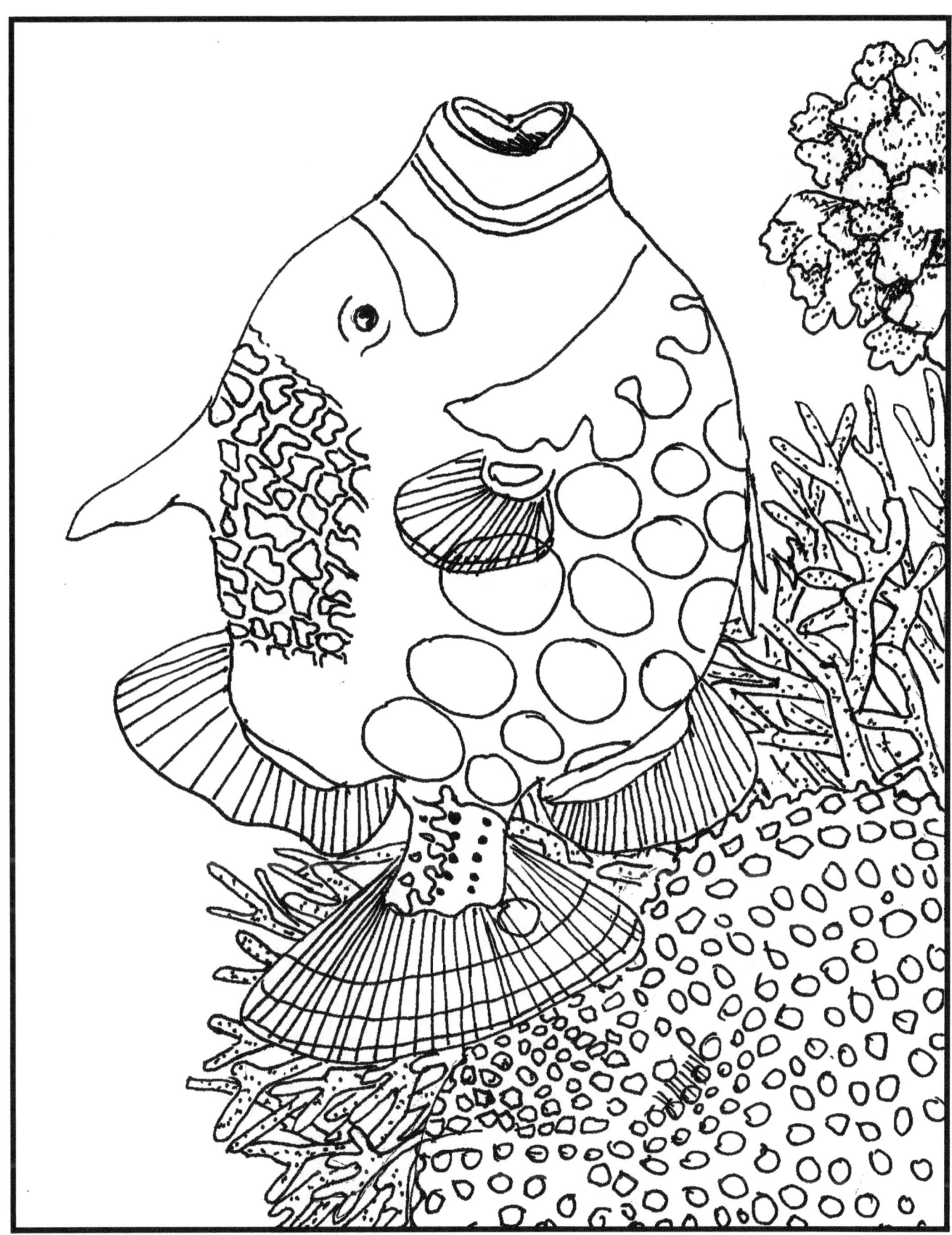

Figure 15 Clown Trigger Fish

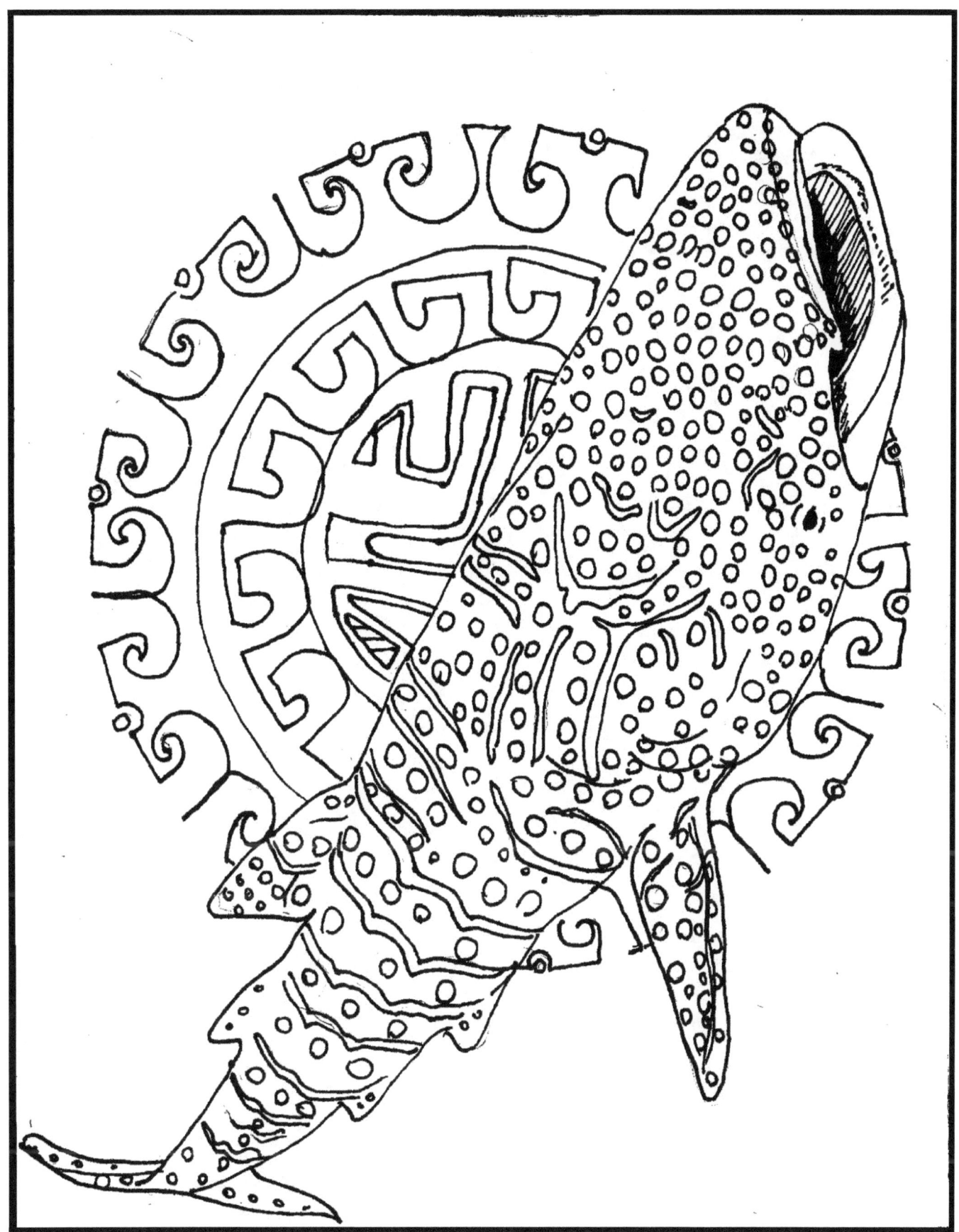

Figure 16 Whale Shark

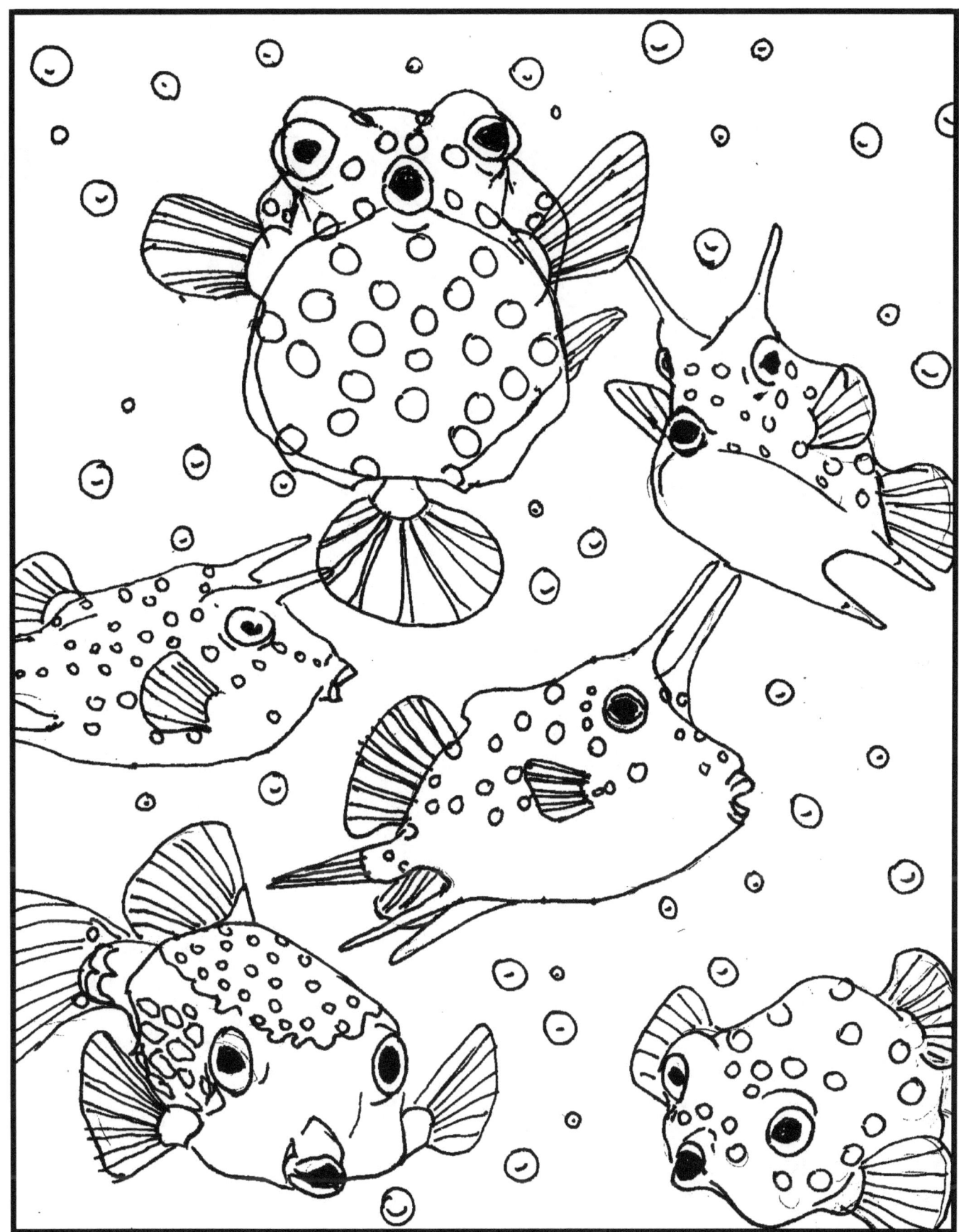

Figure 17 **ox & Cow Fish**

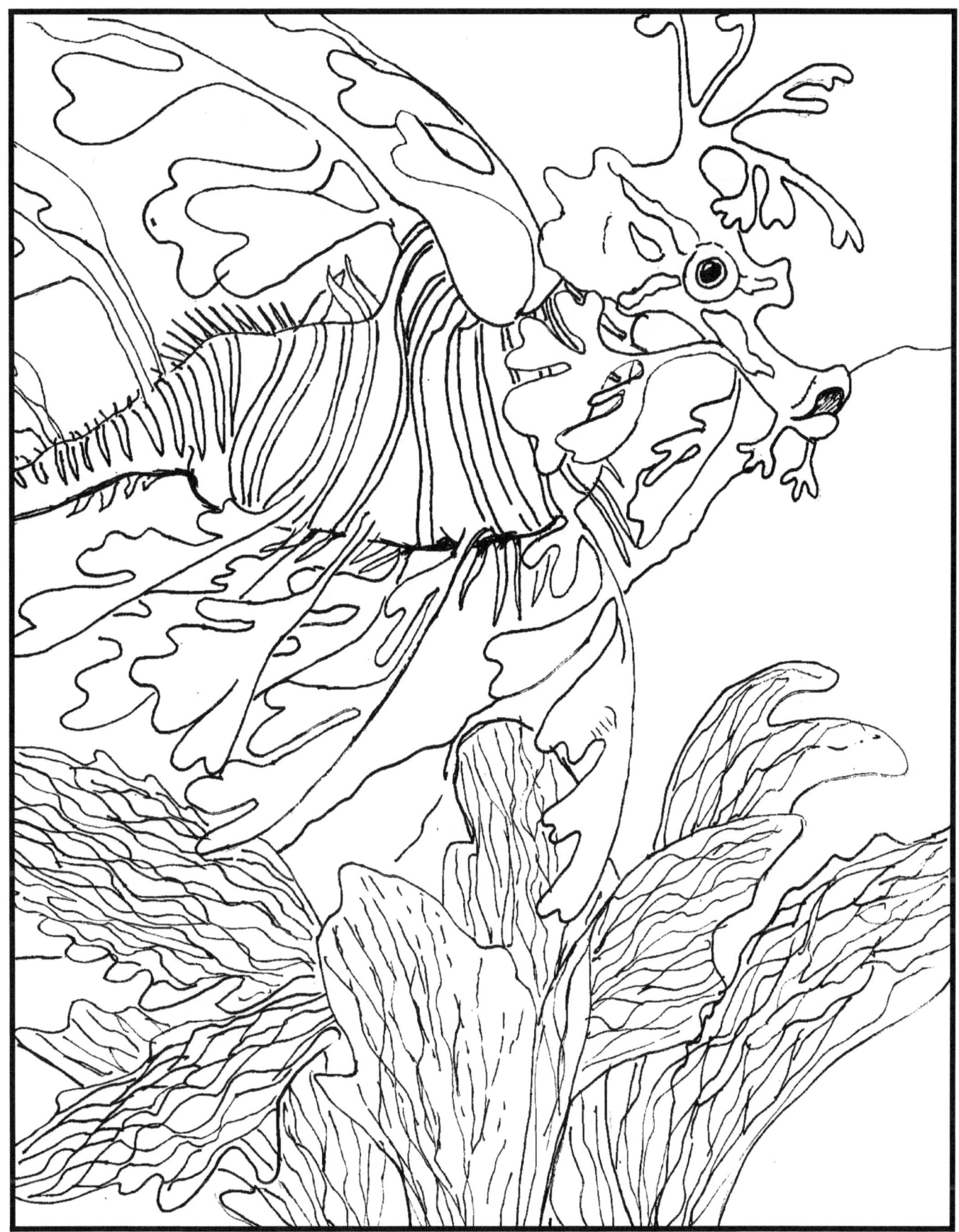

Figure 18 Leafy Sea Dragon

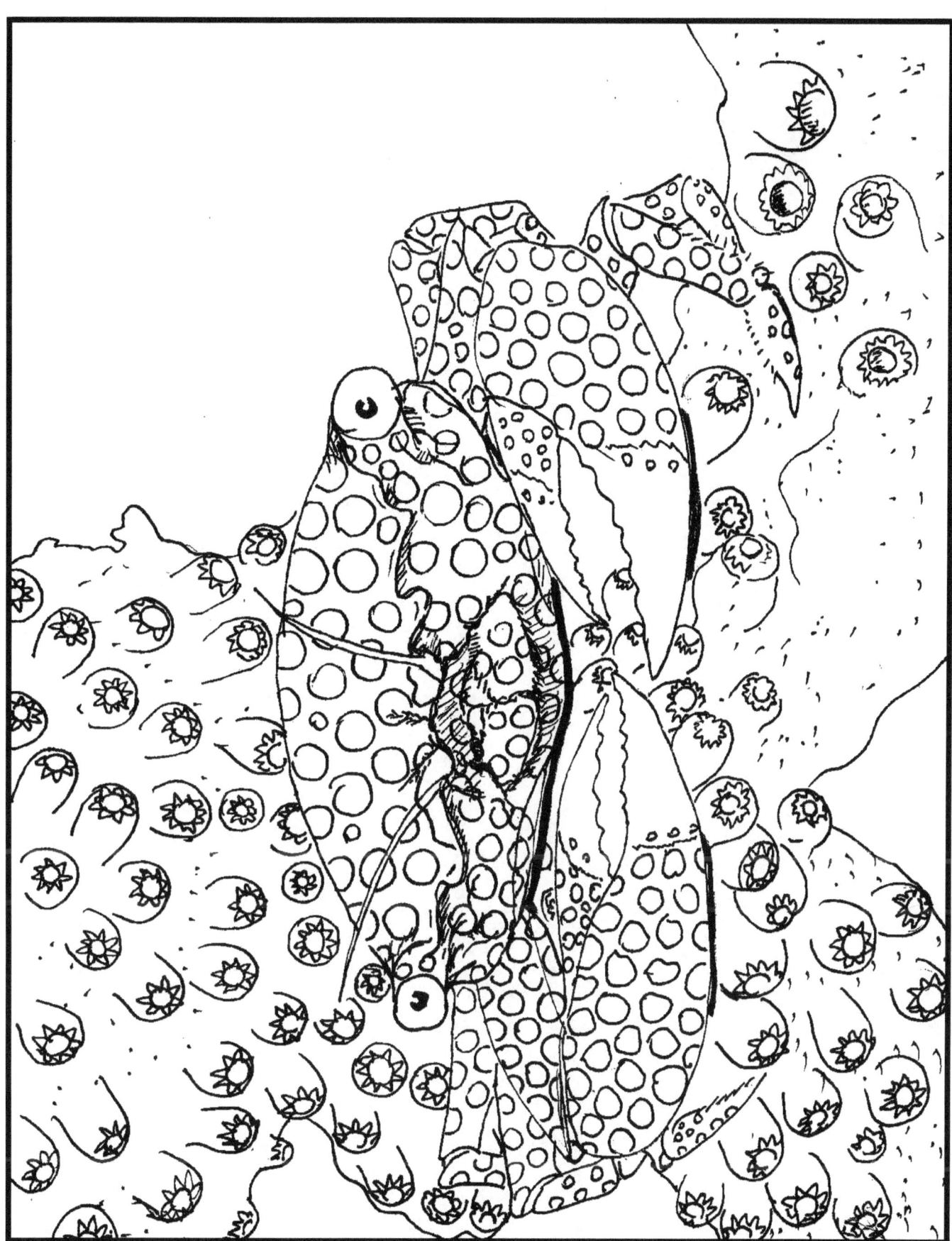

Figure 19 Red Spotted Guard Crab

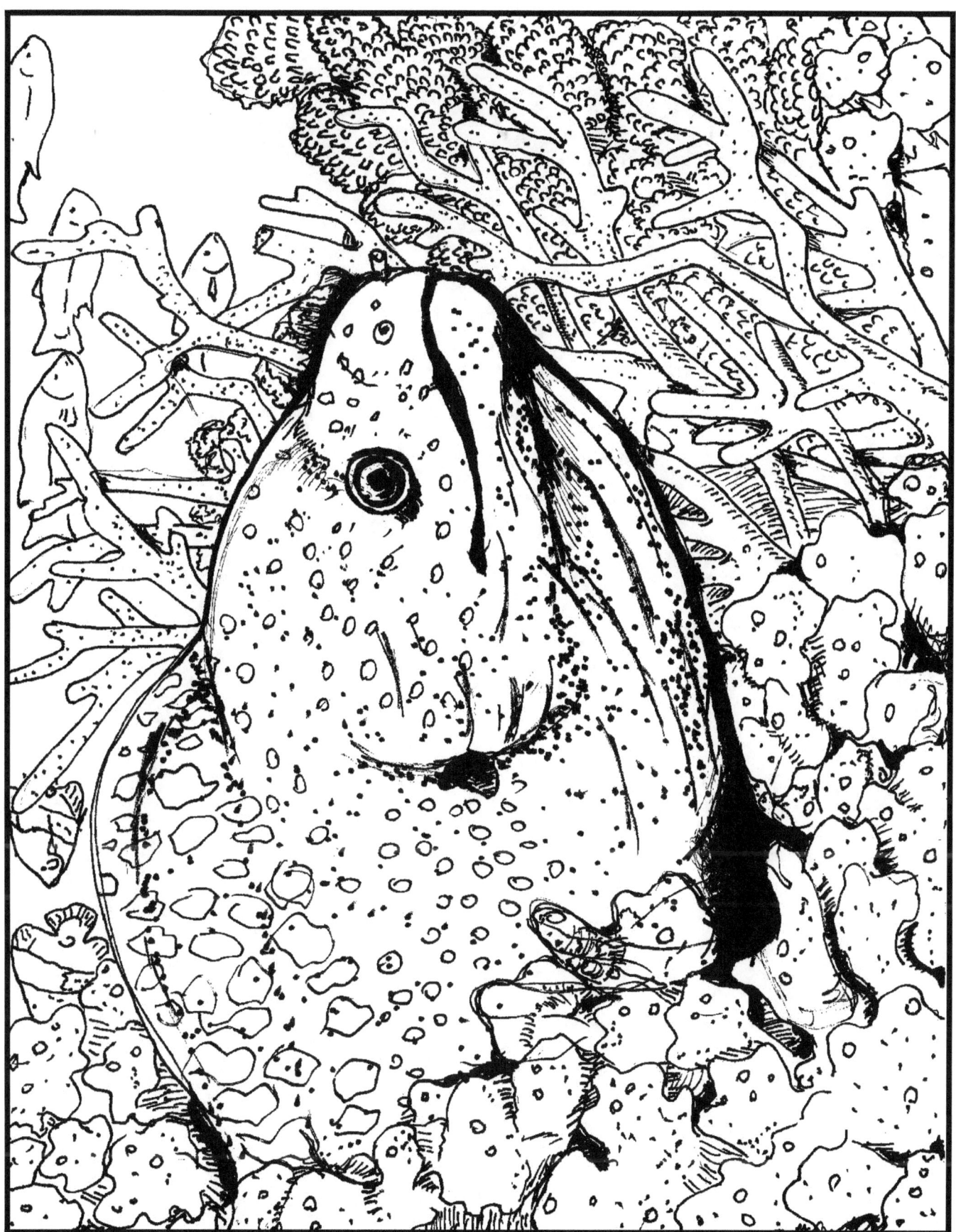

Figure 20 Moray Eel

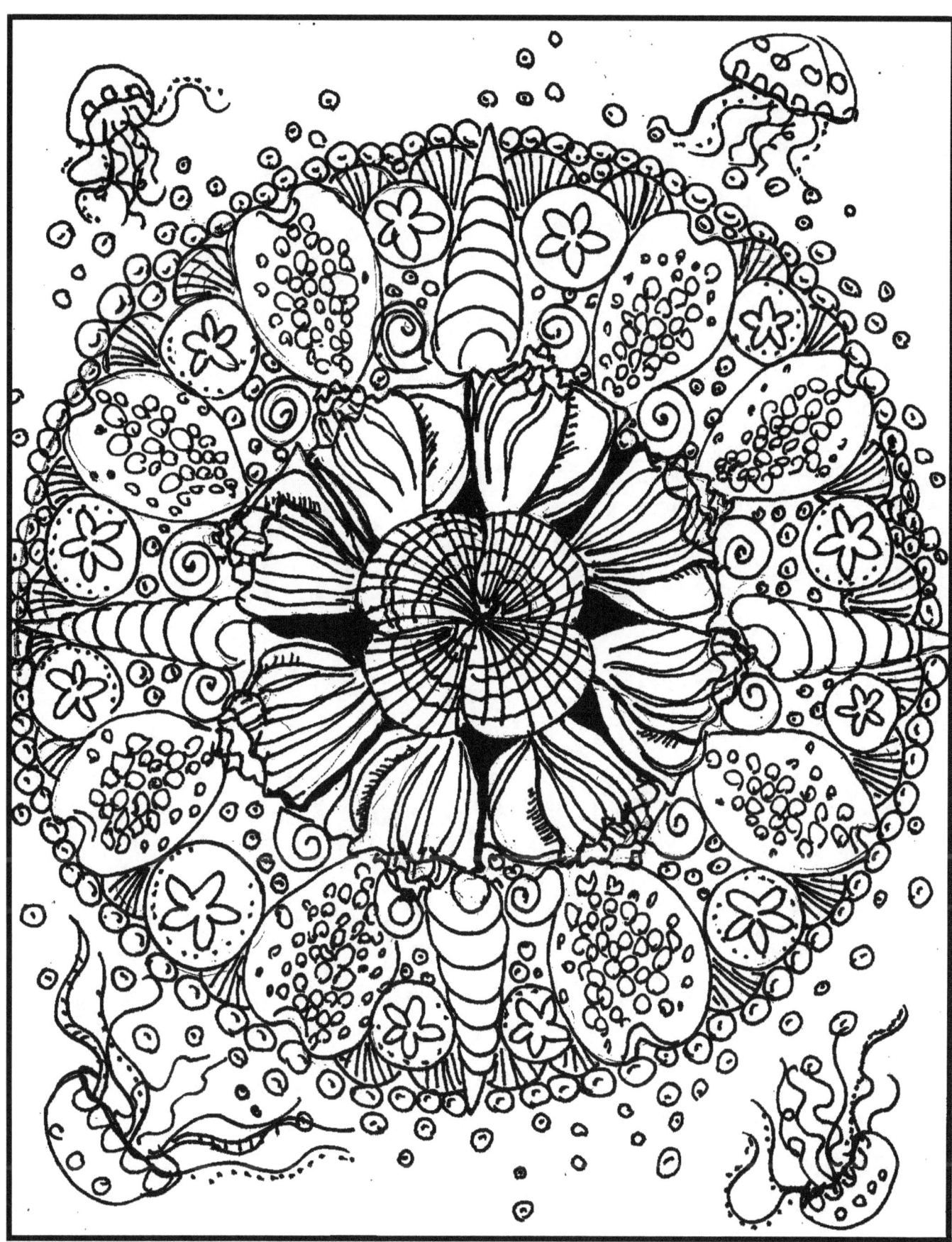

Figure 21 Seashell Mandala

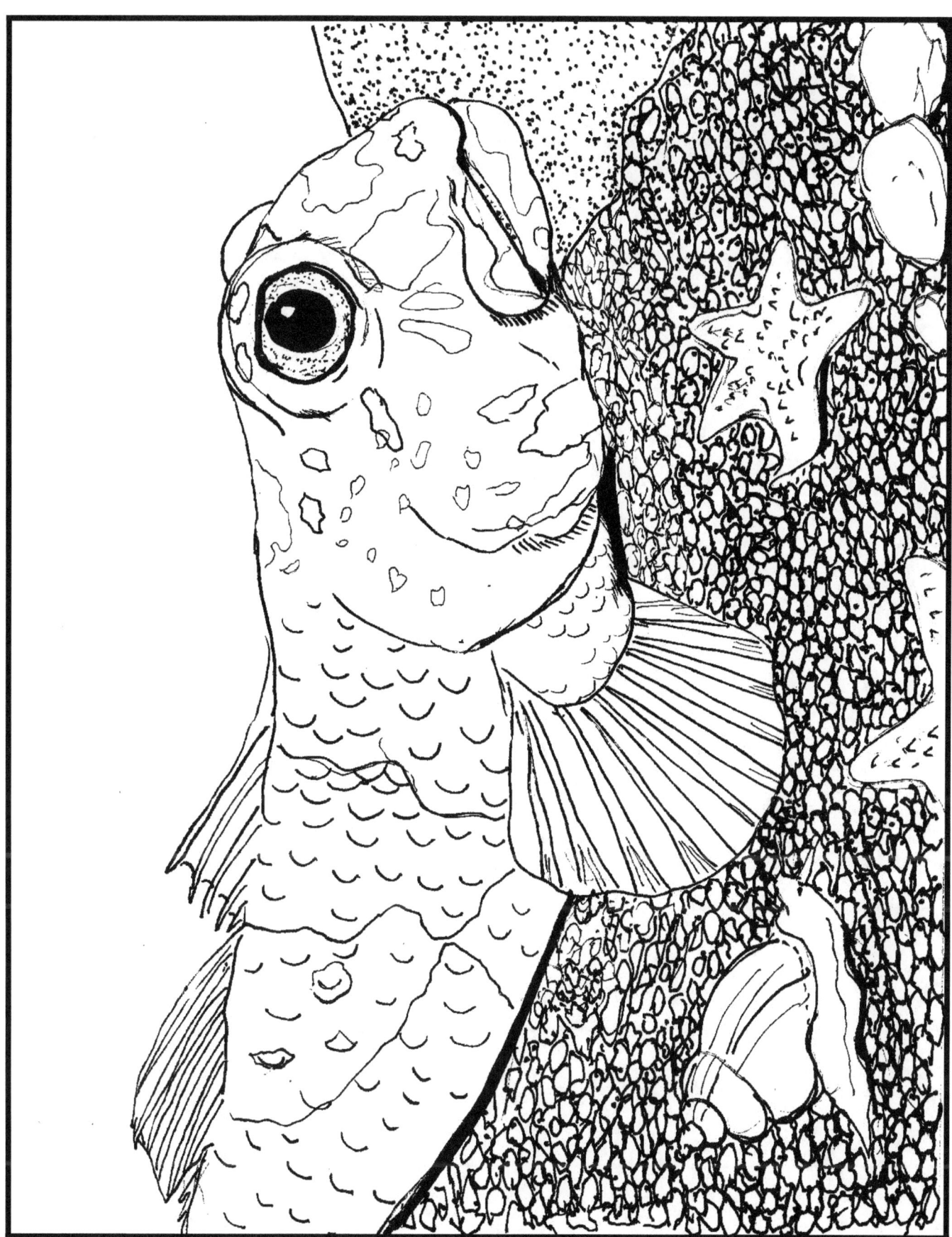

Figure 22 Yellow Arctic Rock cod

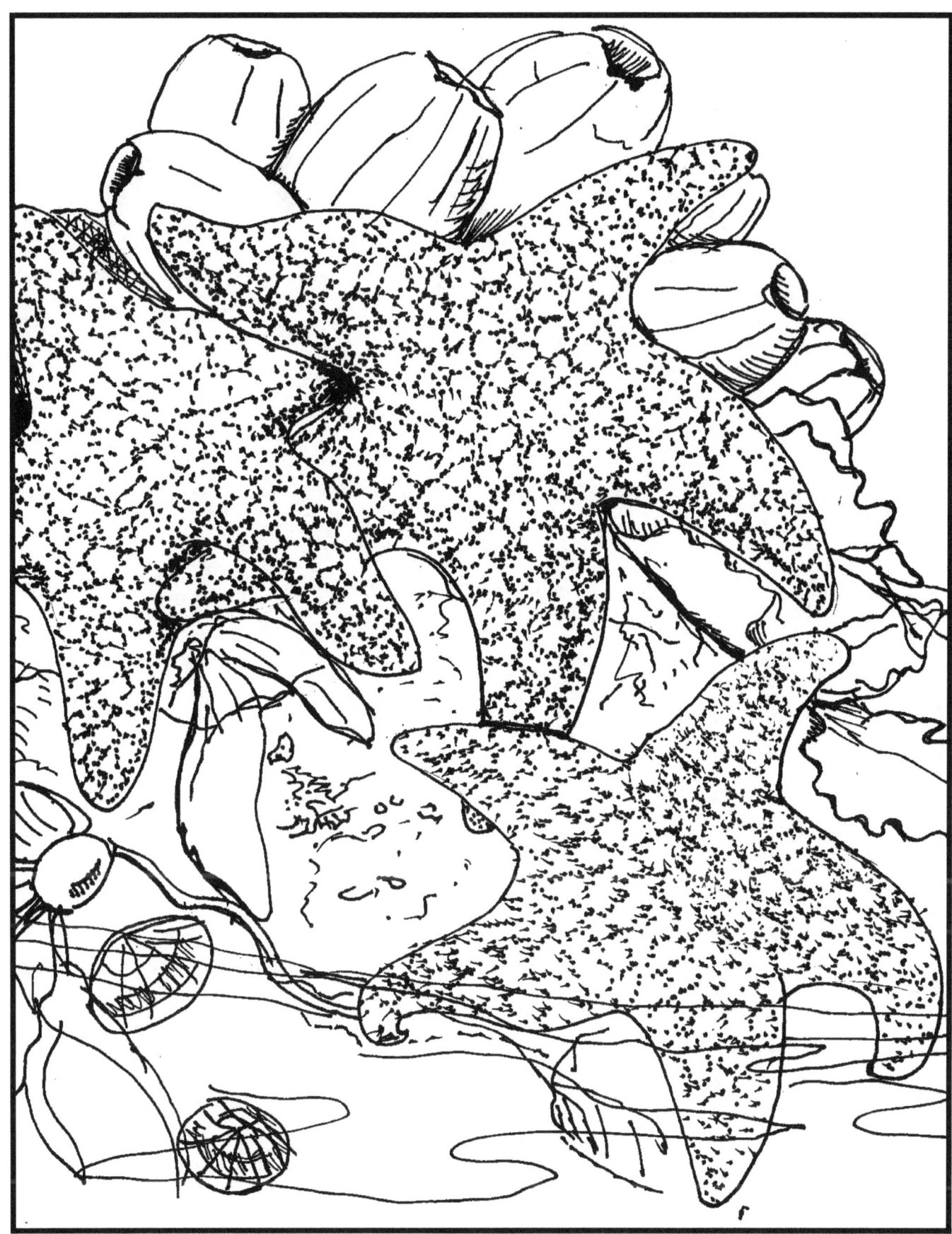

Figure 23 Sea Stars at Low Tide

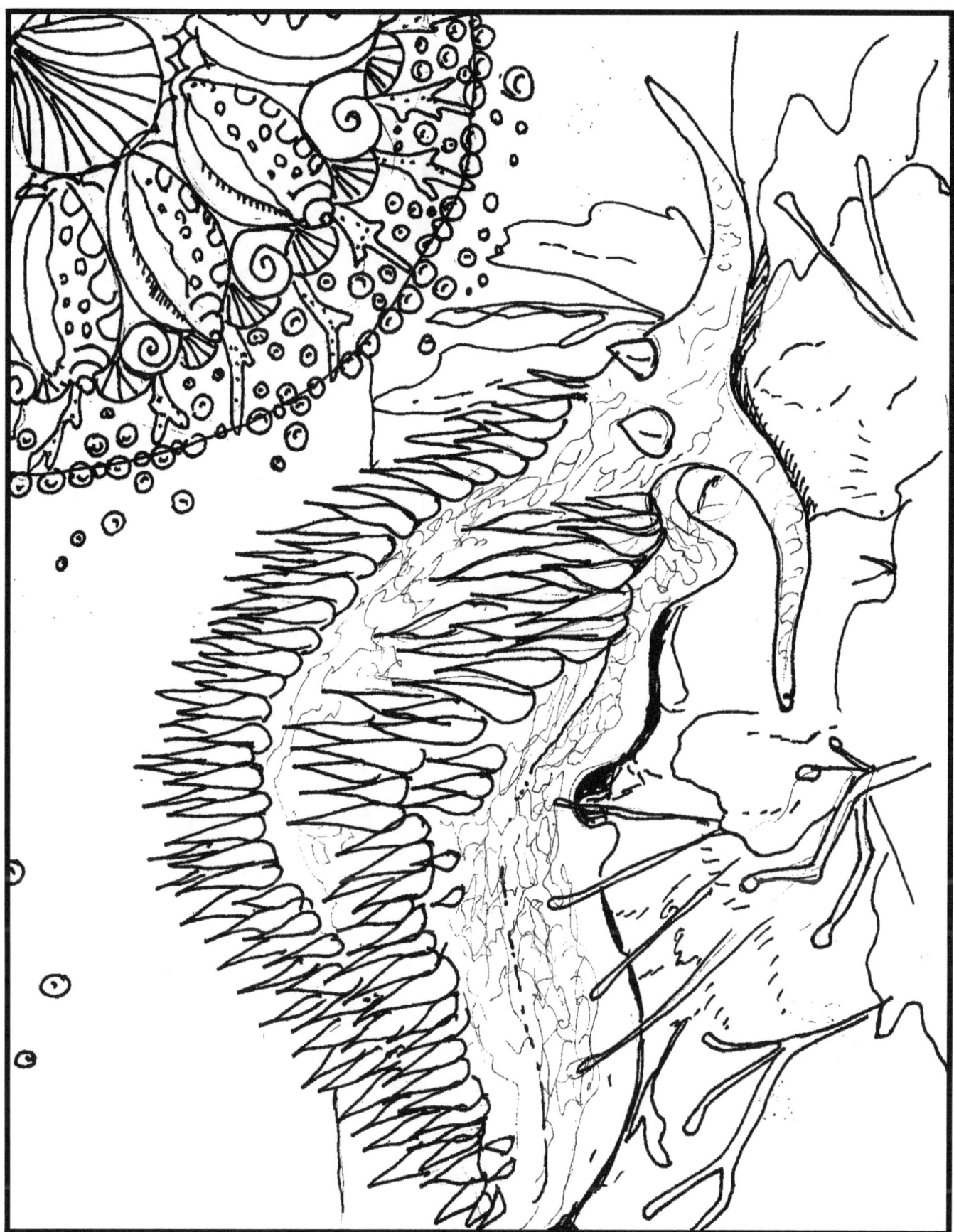

Figure 24 Nudibranch

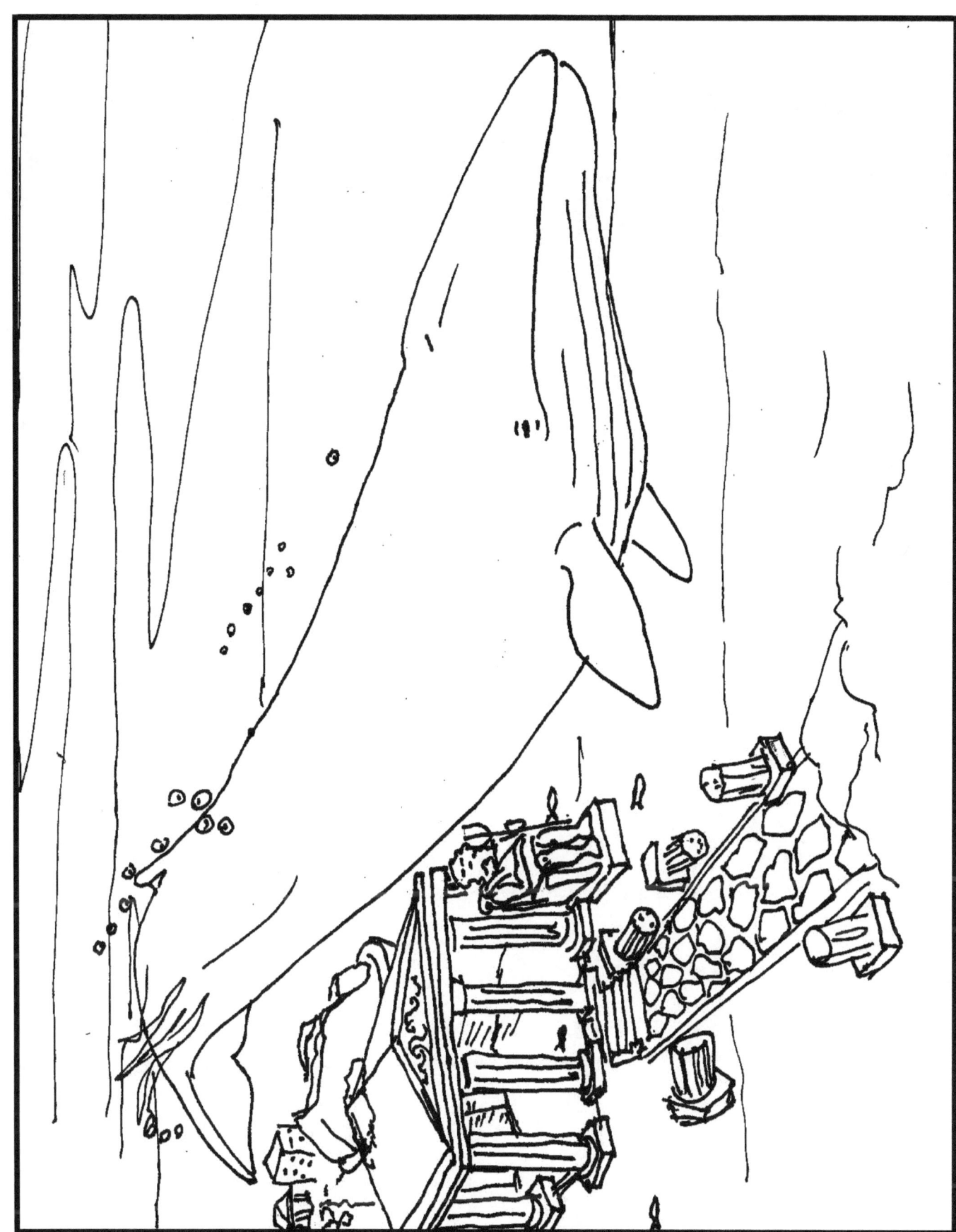

Figure 25 Blue Whale Swimming Over Atlantis

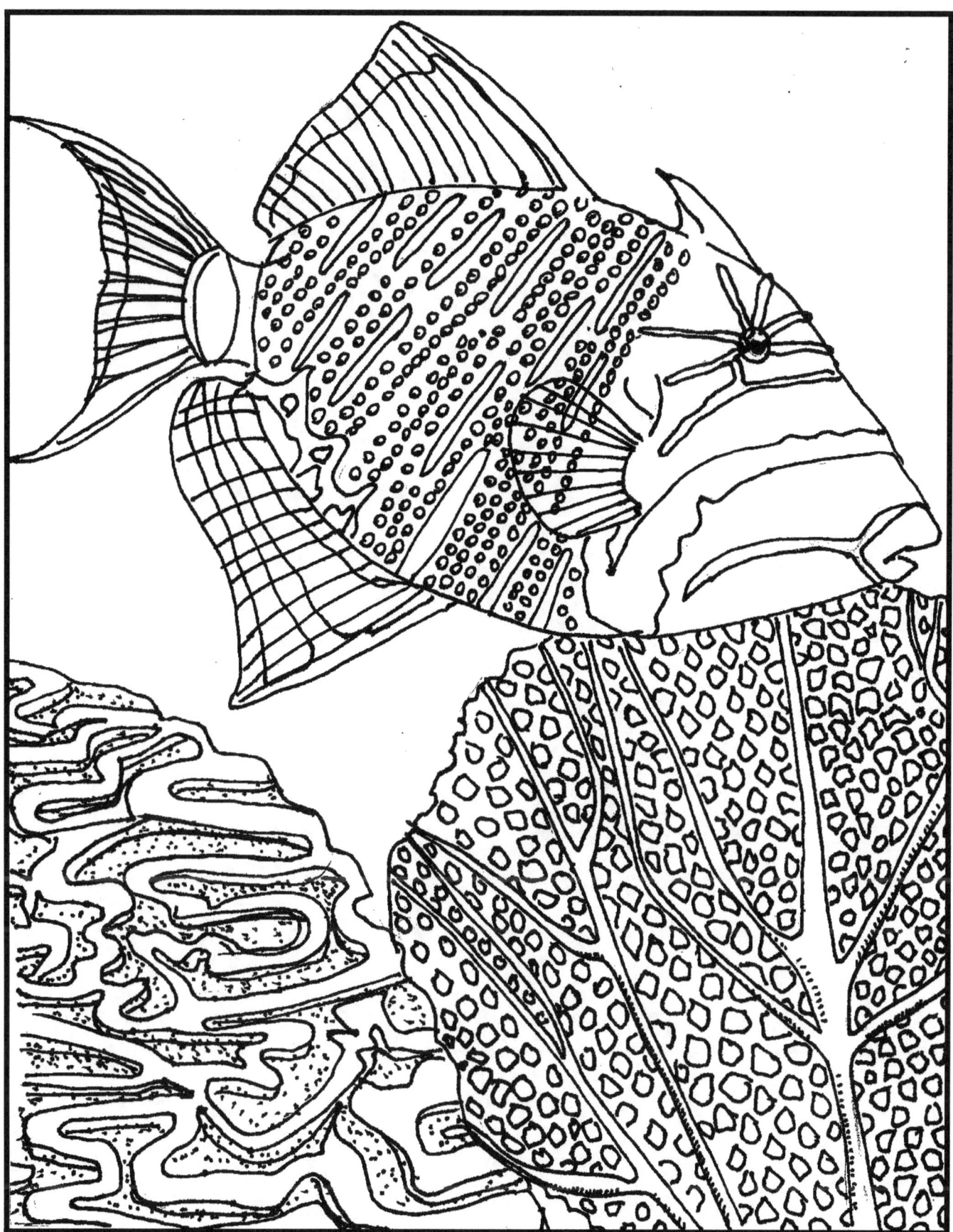

Figure 26 Queen Trigger Fish

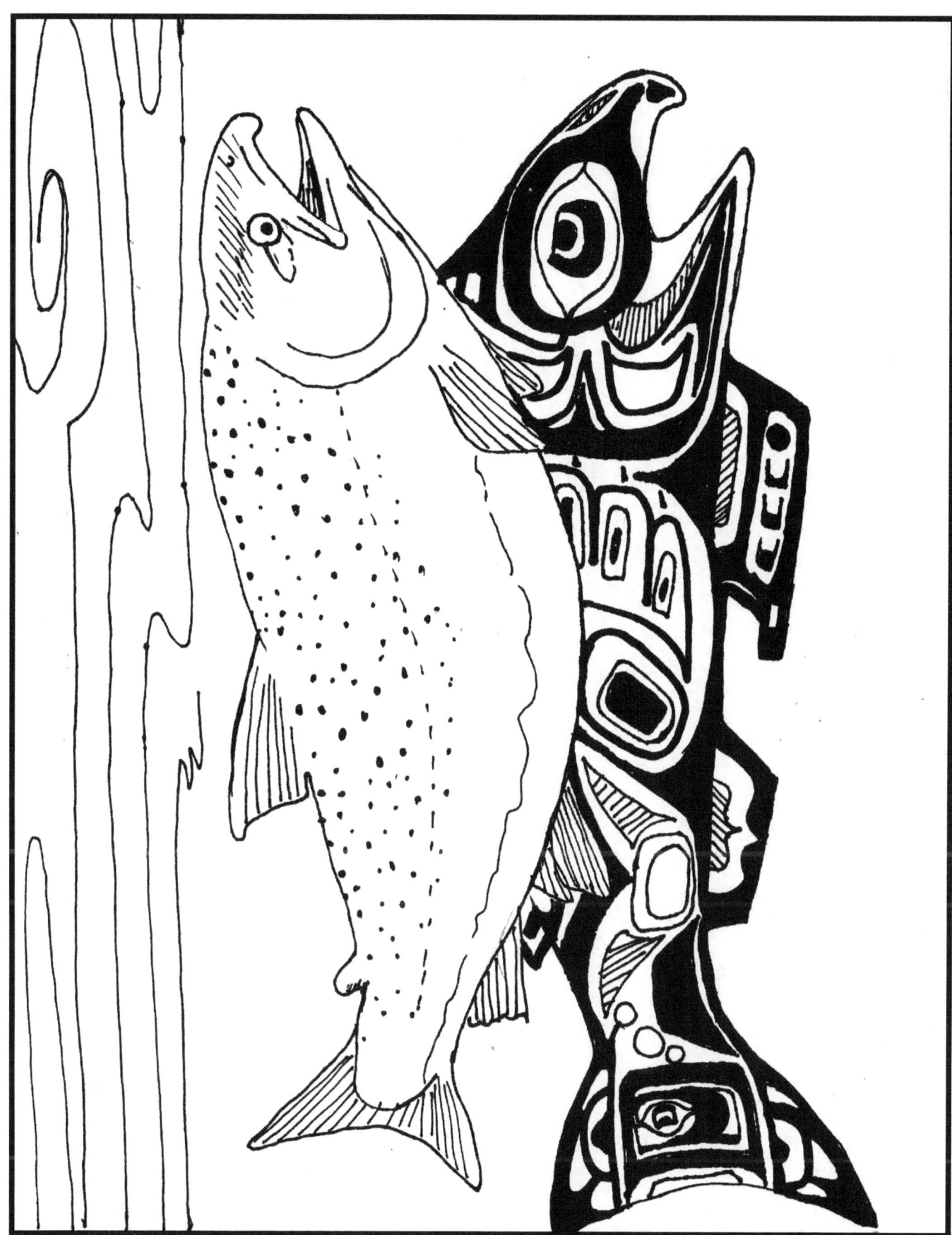

Figure 27 Salmon

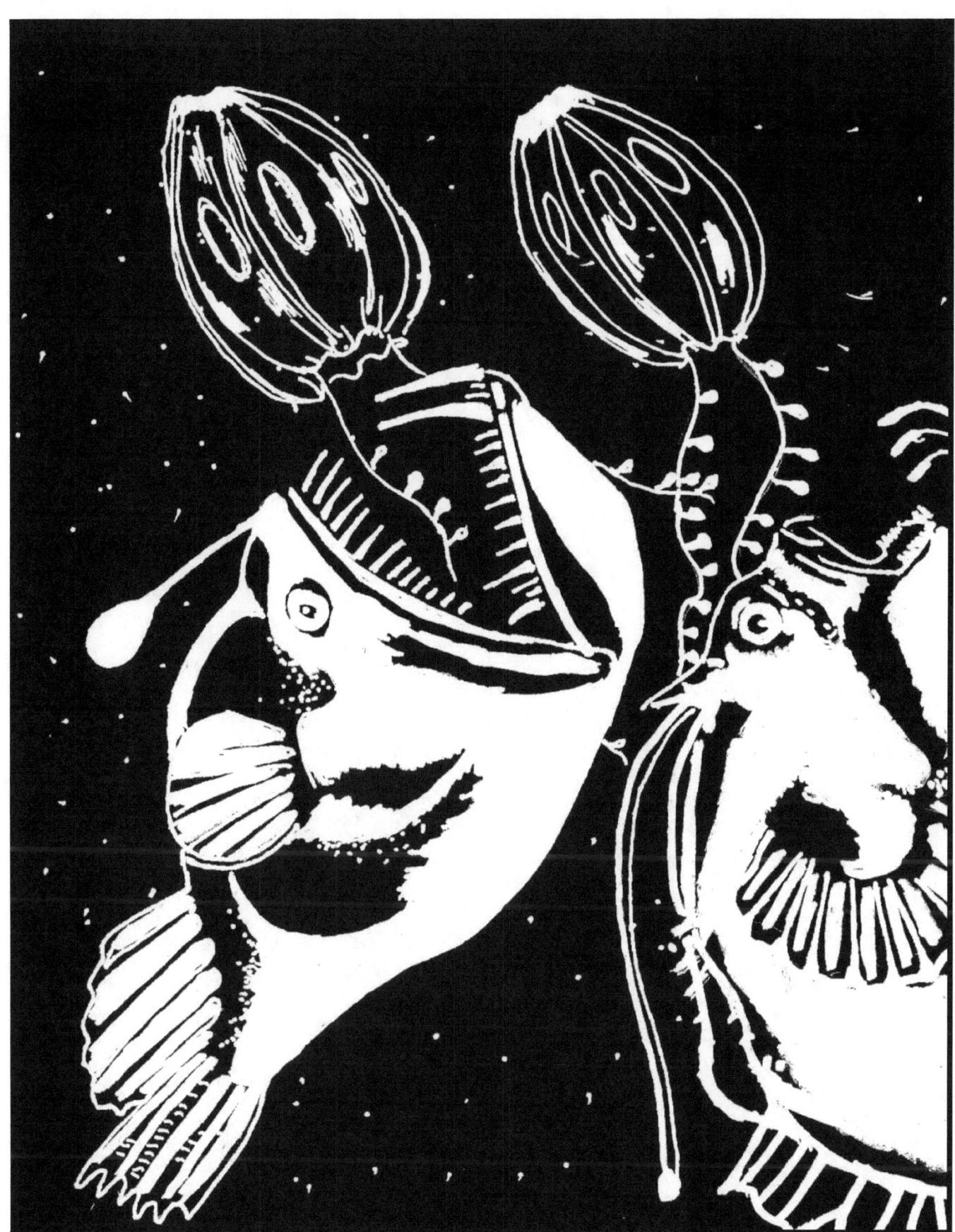

Figure 28 Who Needs Aliens?

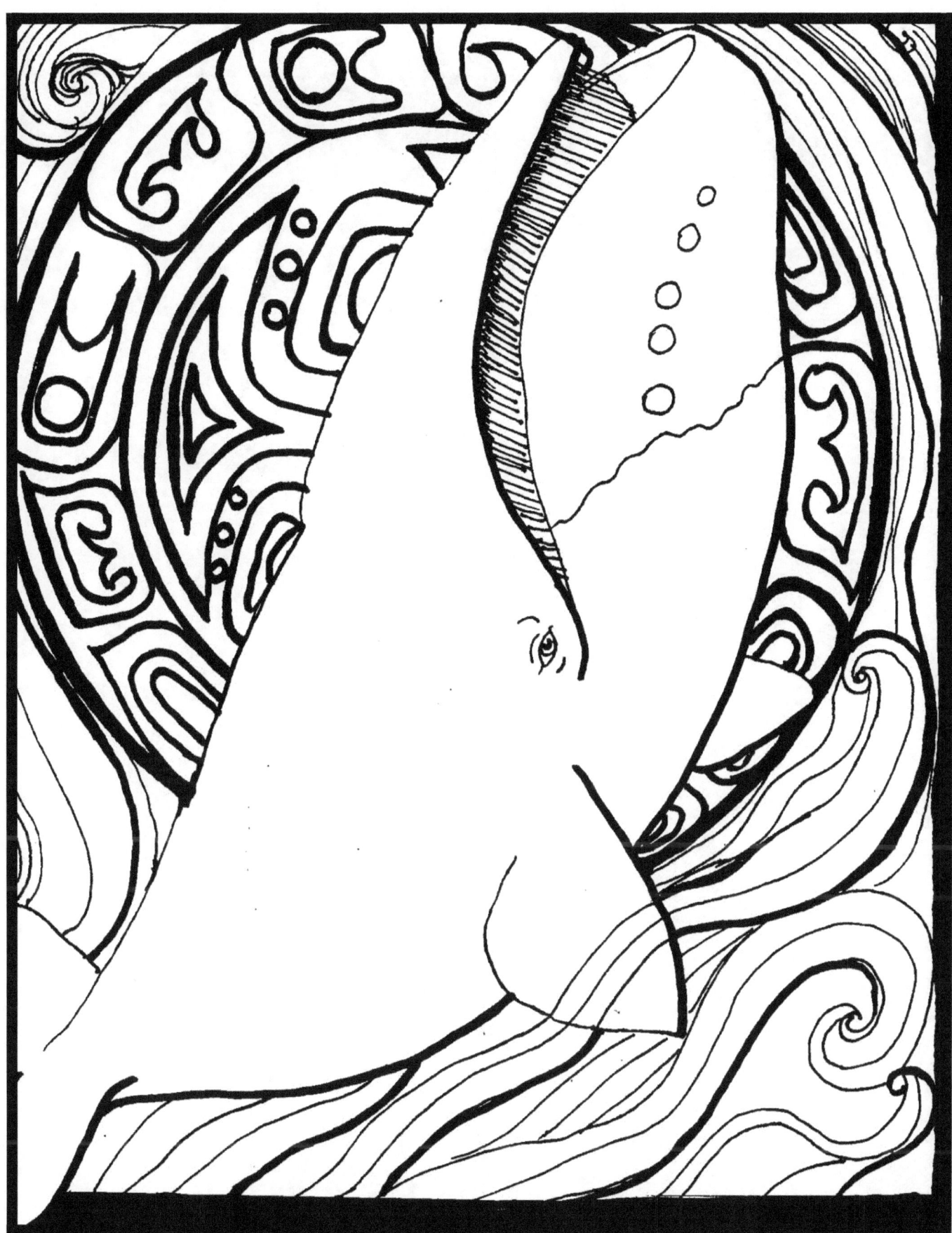

Figure 29 Bowhead Whale

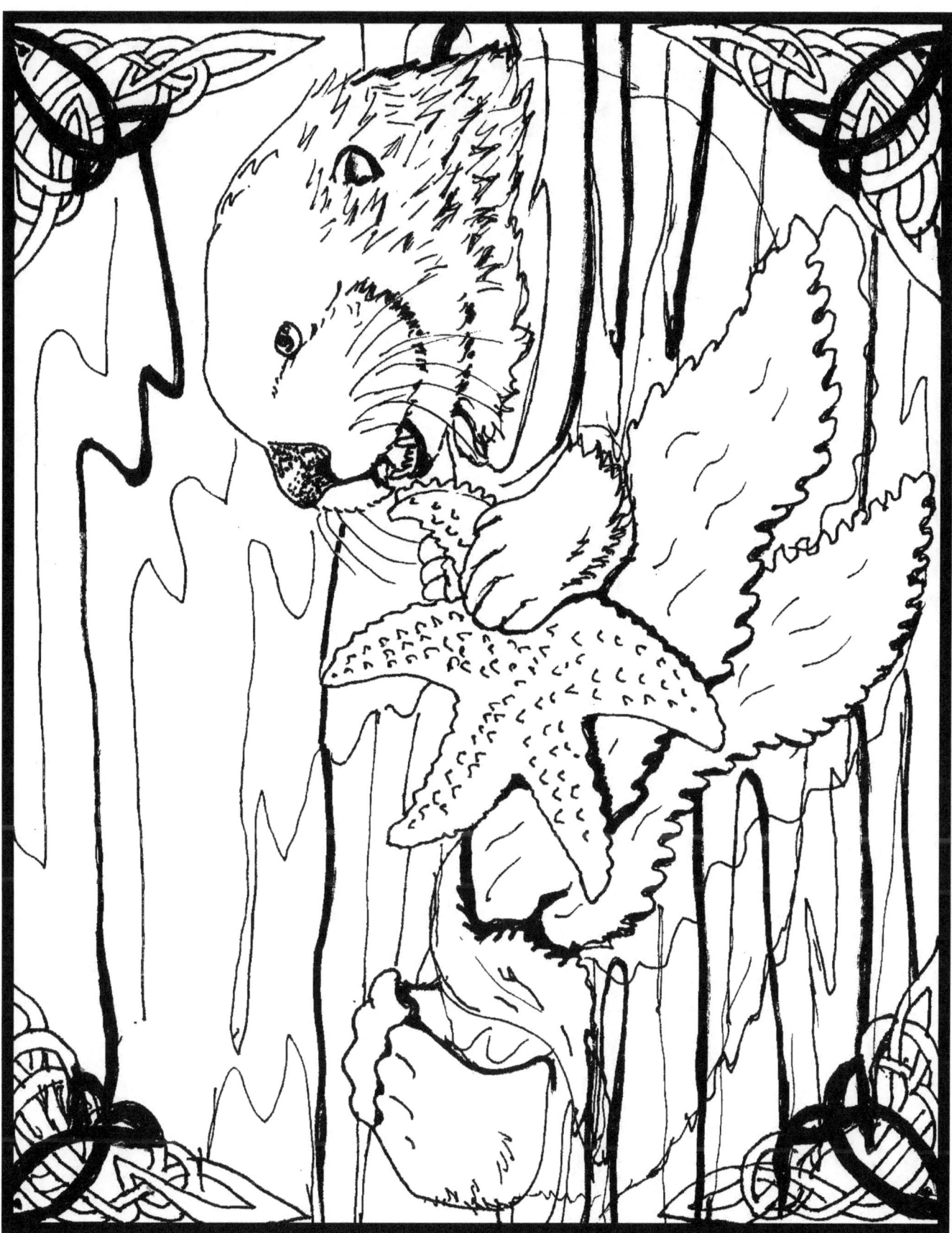

Figure 30 Sea Otter

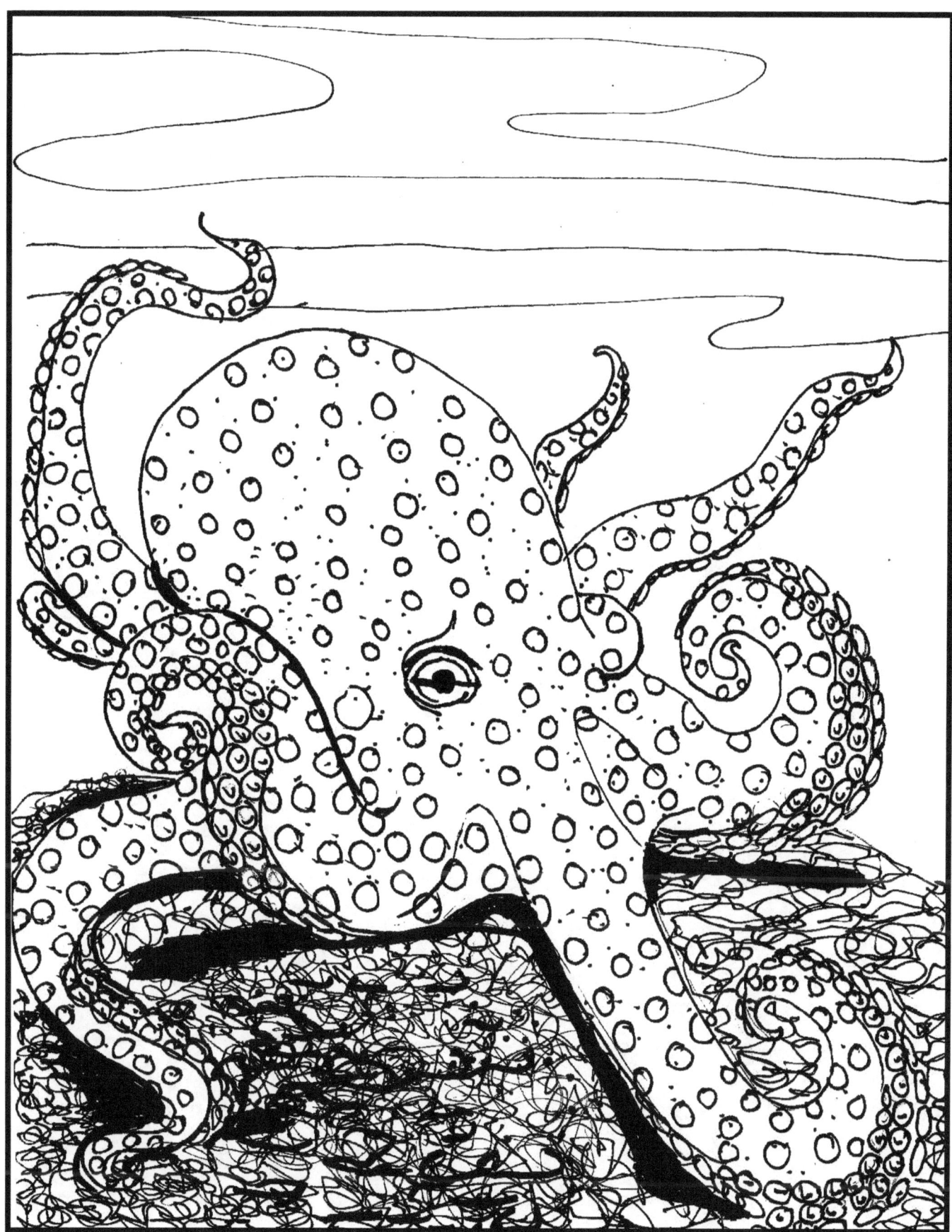

Figure 31 Octopus

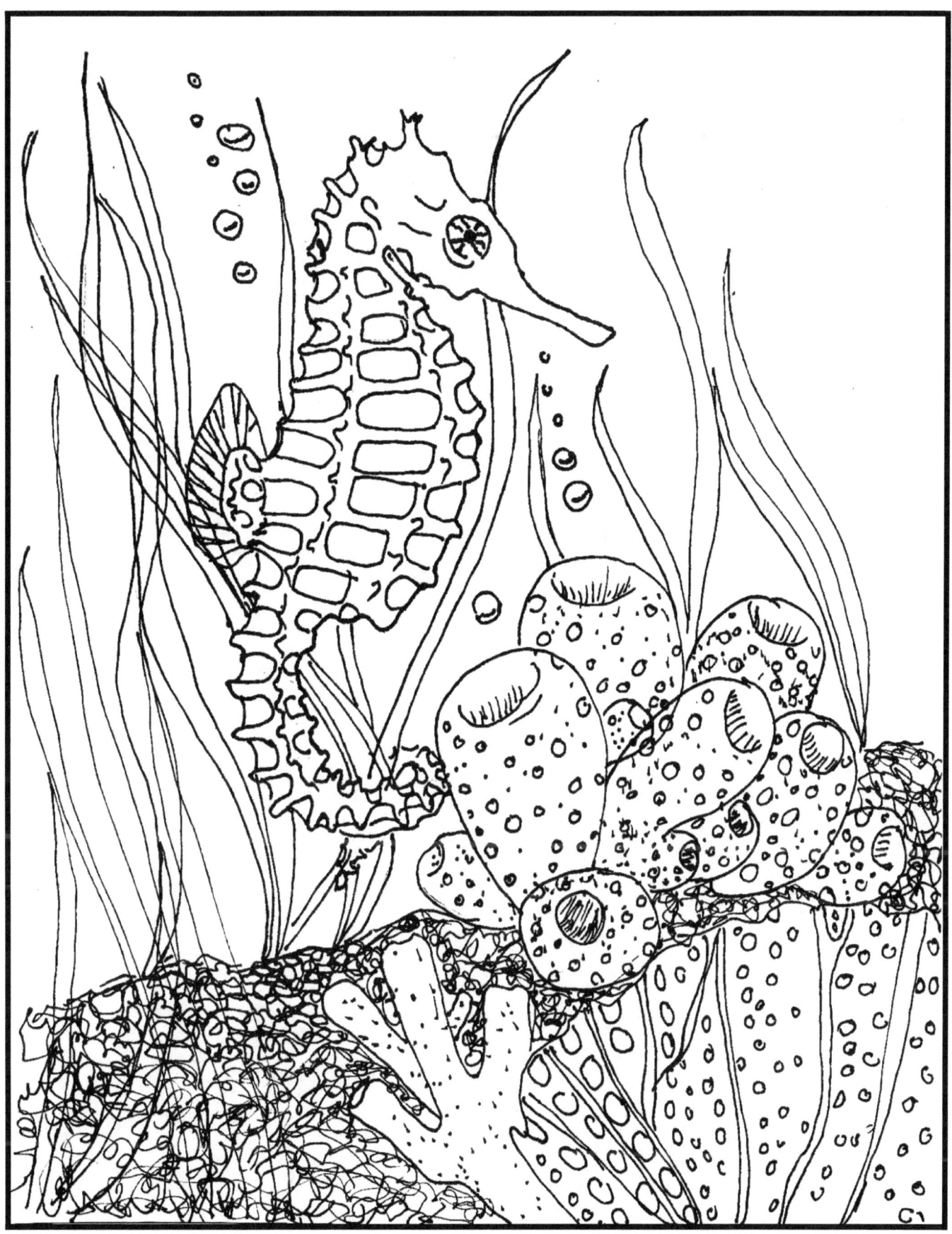

Figure 32 Seahorse

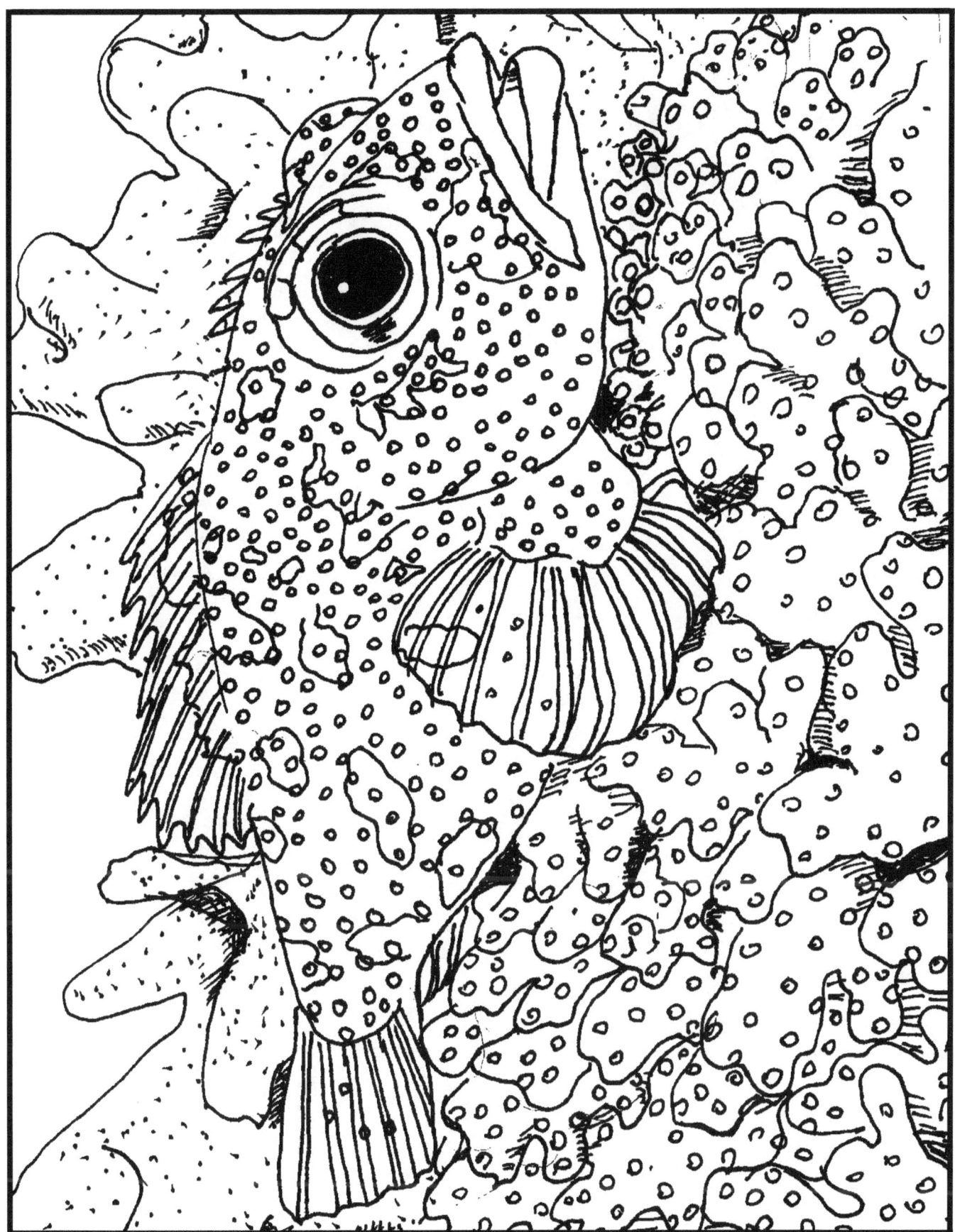

Figure 33 Yellow Spotted Scorpion Fish

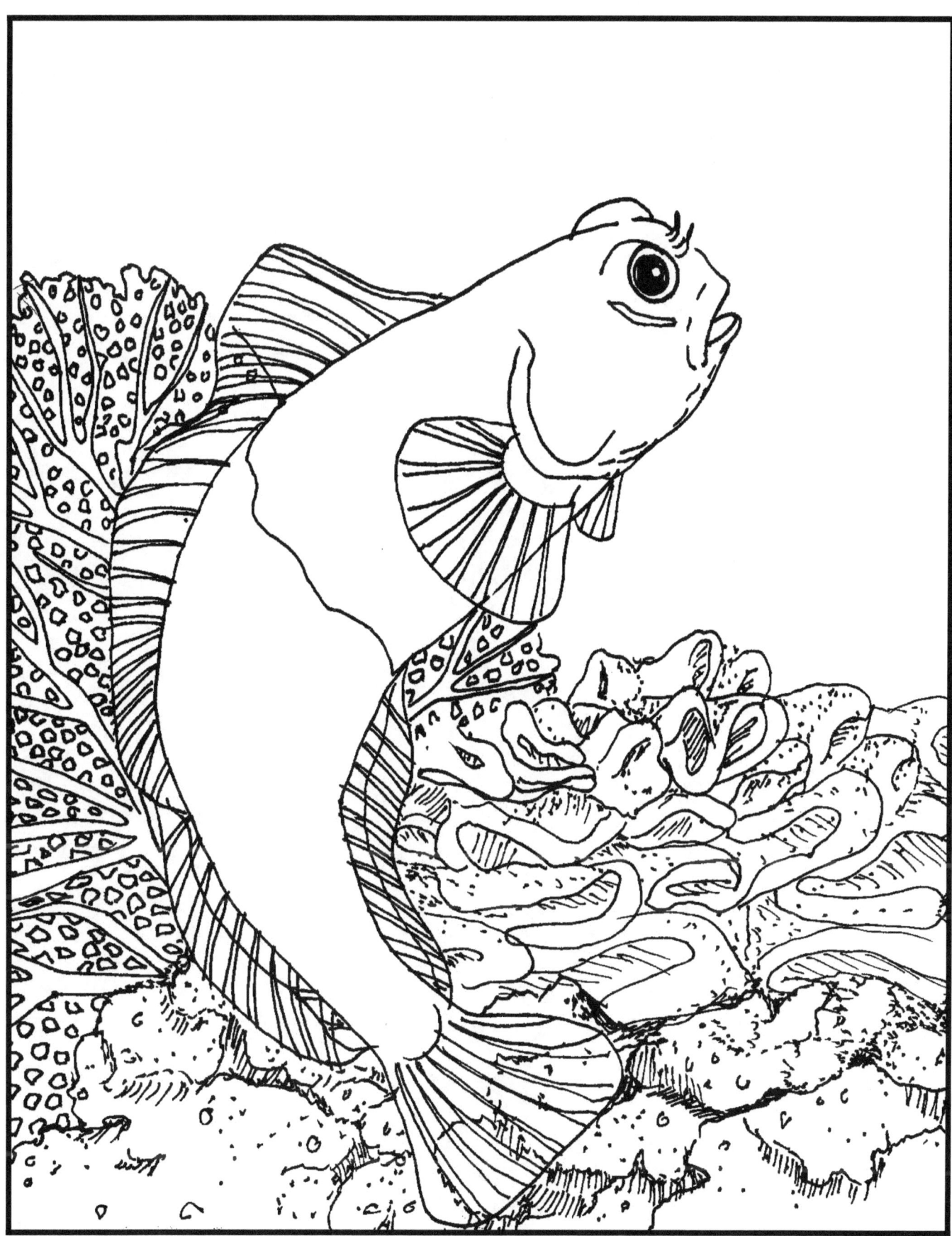

Figure 34 Bicolor Blenny

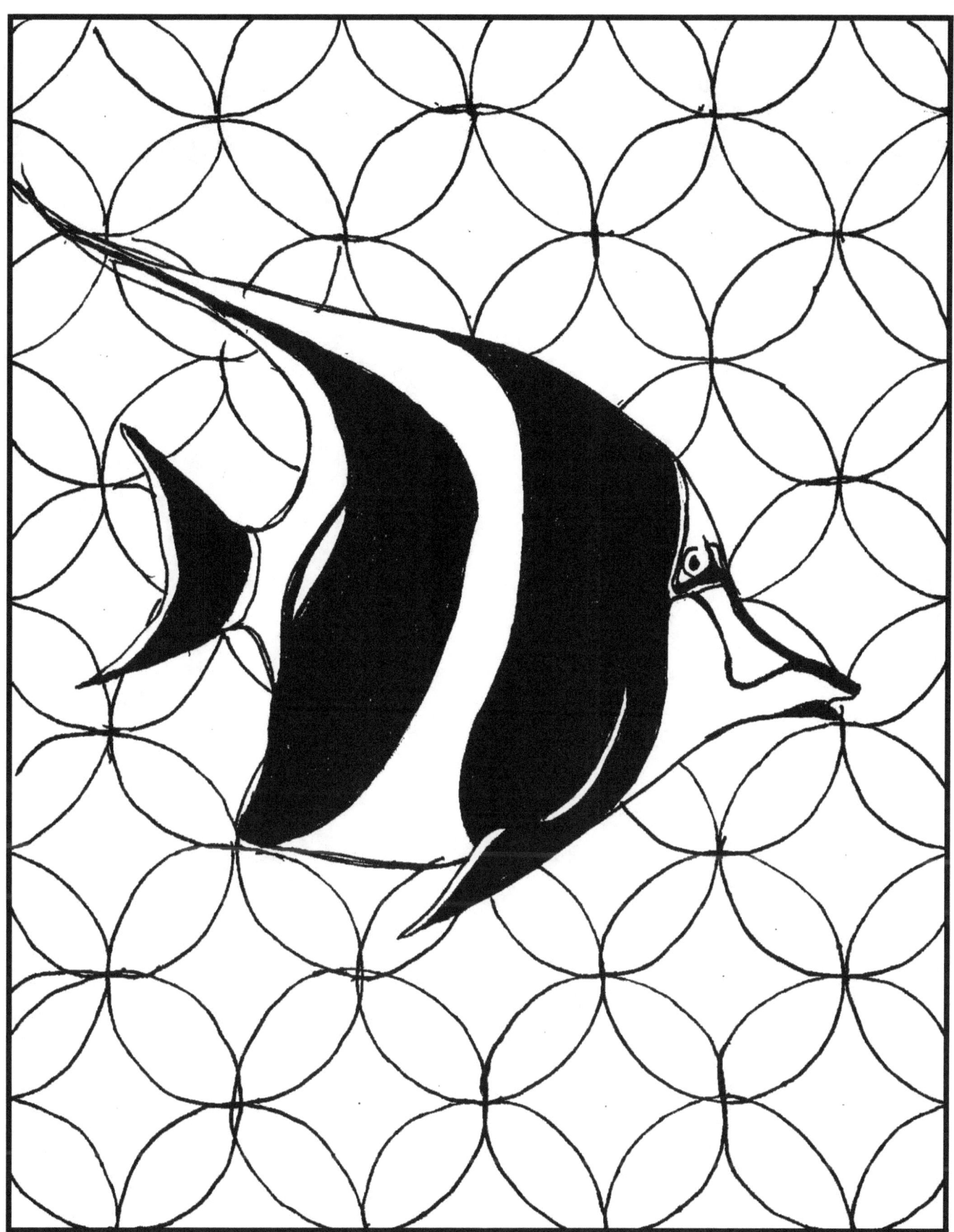

Figure 35 Moorish Idol

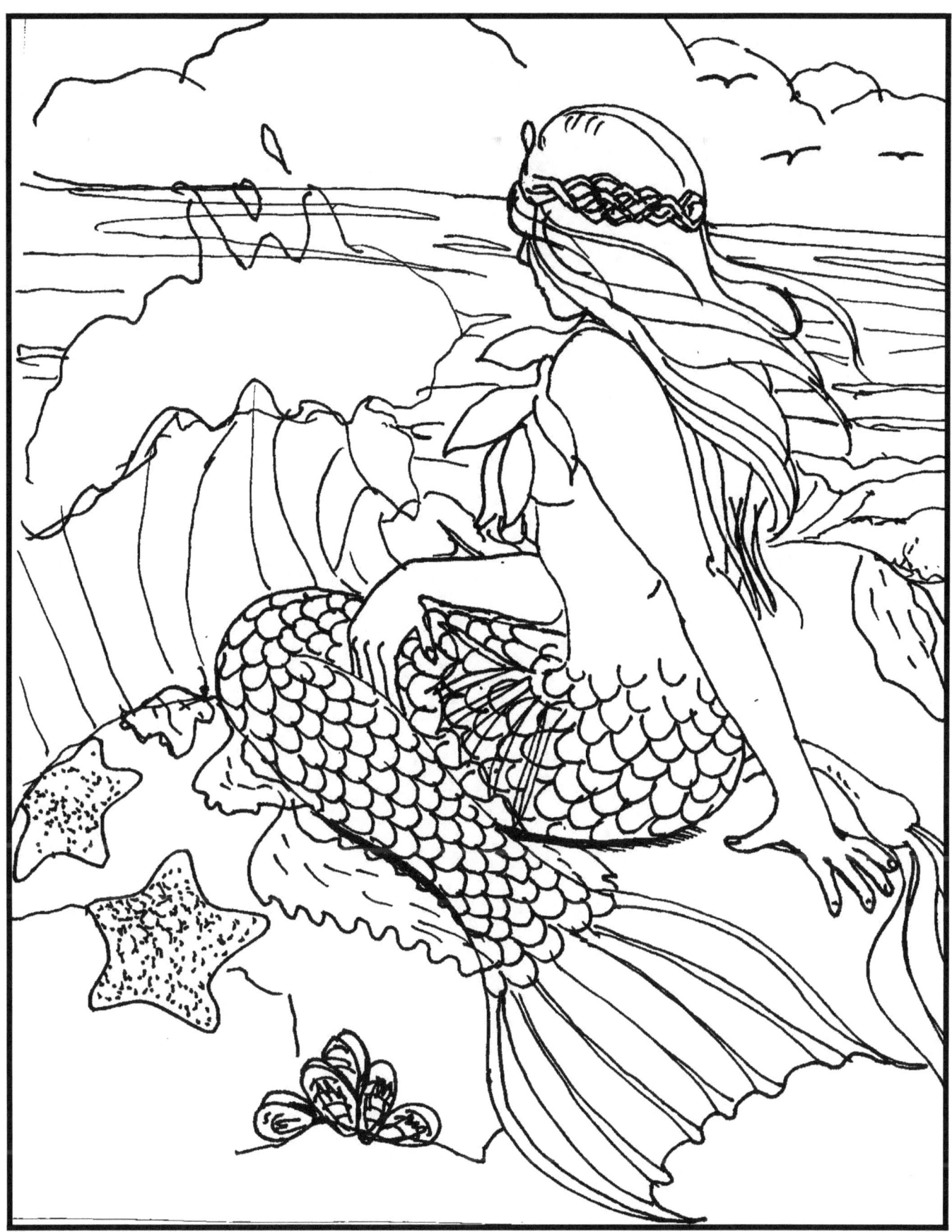

Figure 36 Resting on the Rock

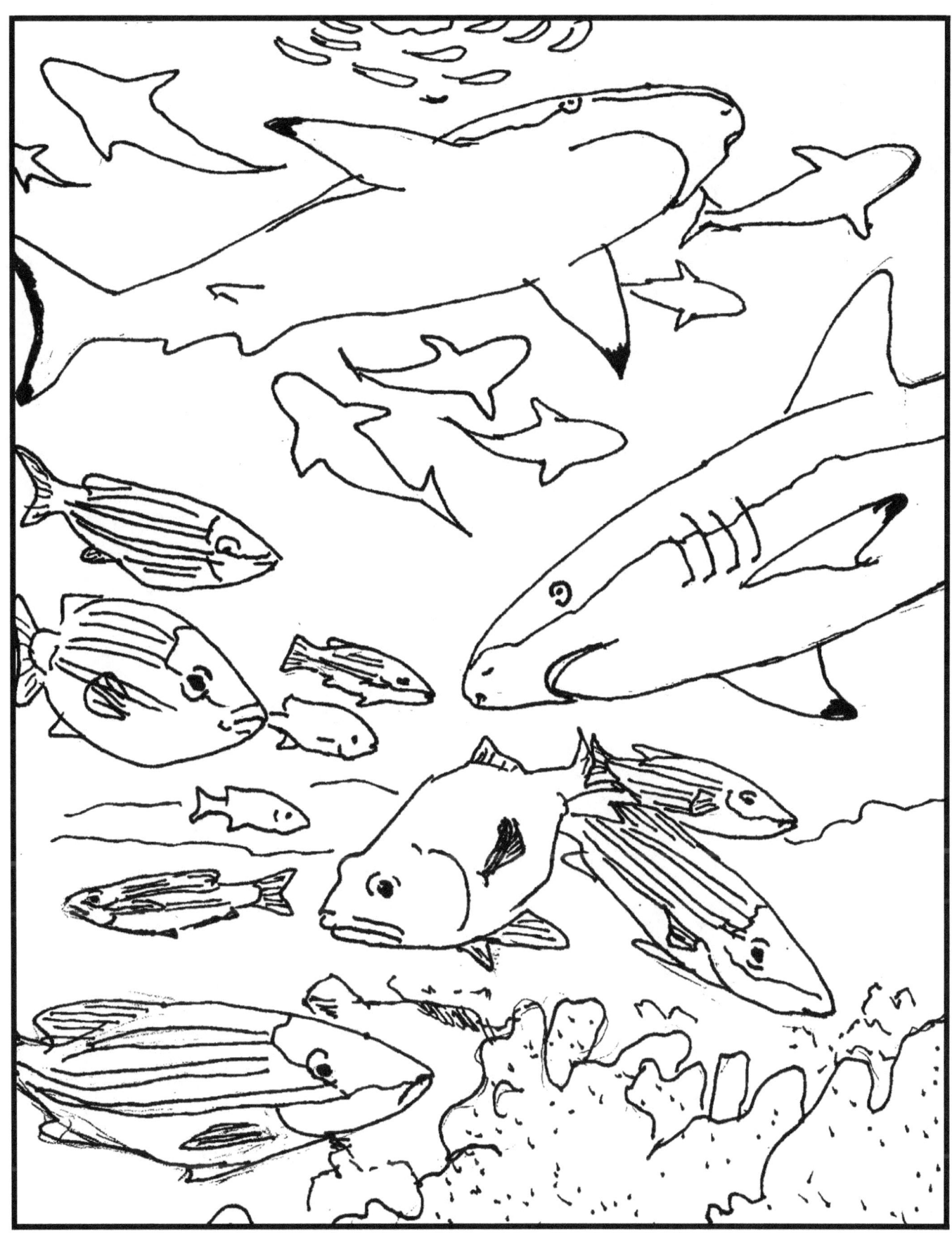

Figure 37 Swimming with the Sharks

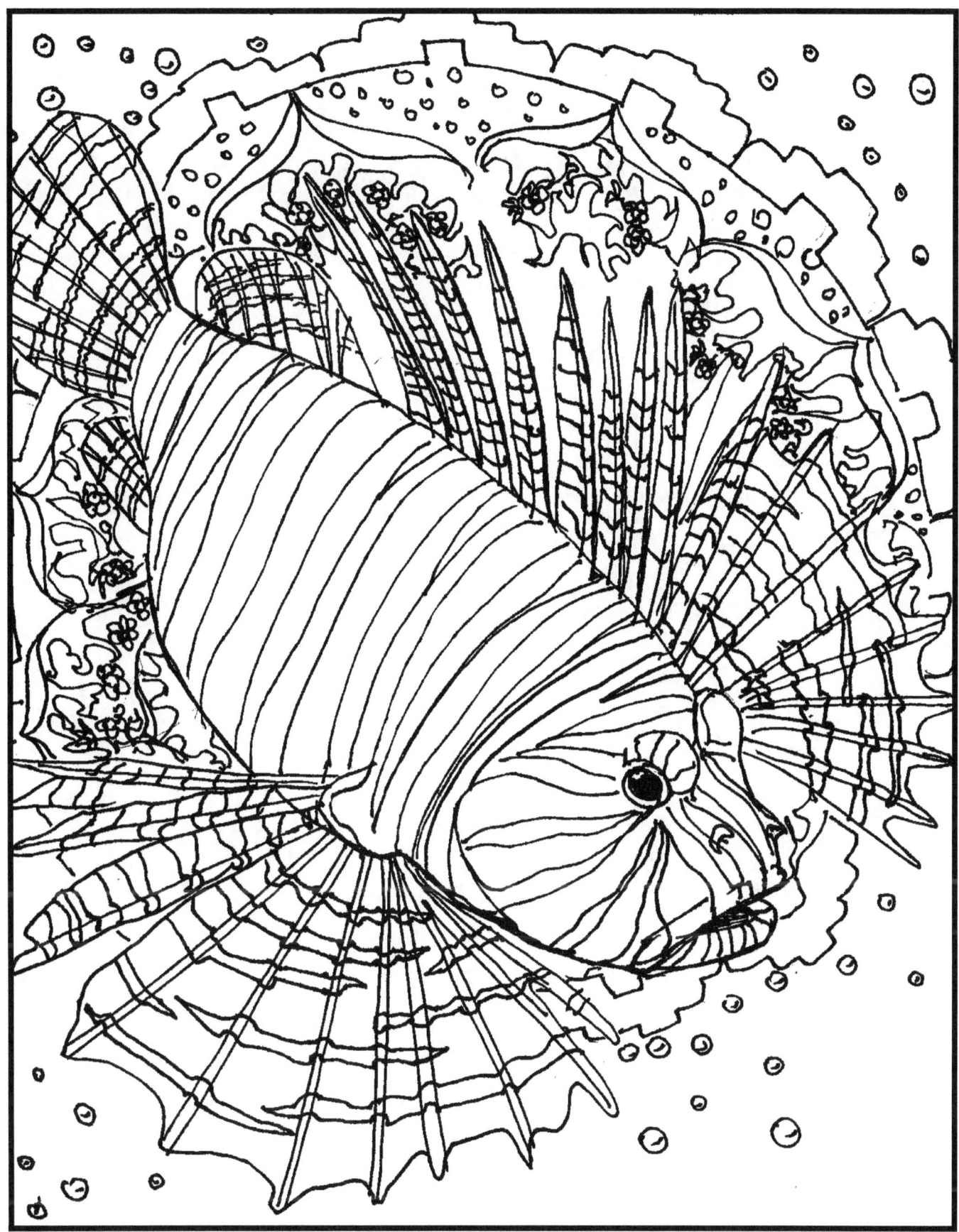

Figure 38 Lion Fish

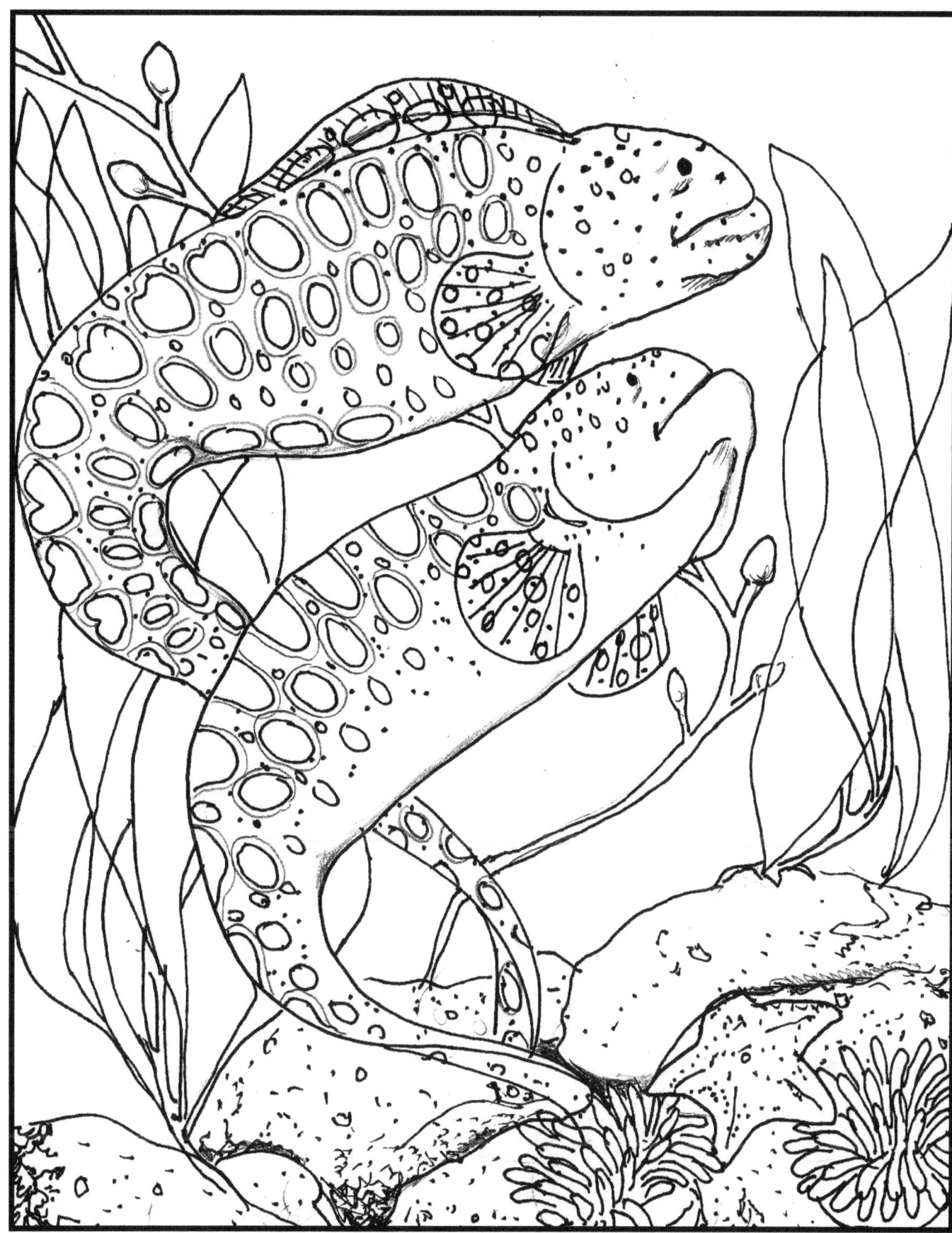

Figure 39 Wolf Eels

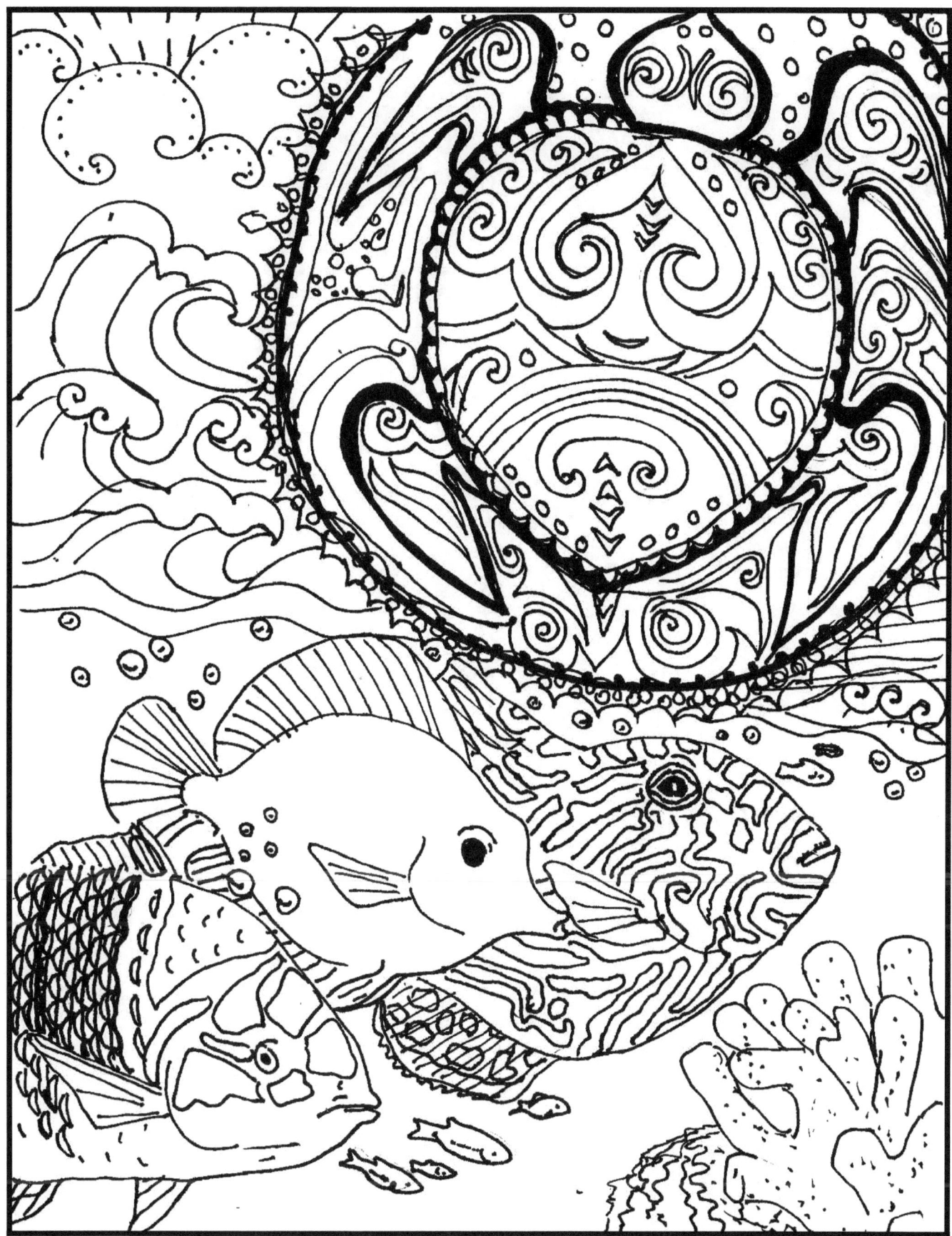

Figure 40 Three Amigos